MY TAKE

3

RAFAEL E. EVANGELISTA

JUNE 2023

Published in USA in June 2023 by
TATAY JOBO ELIZES,
Self-Publisher, under the permission and
authorization of

RAFAEL E. EVANGELISTA
author and copyright owner.

The copyright owner can withdraw this permission
at his discretion without any objection from Tatay
Jobo Elizes at any time. Printing of this book is
using the present day method of Print-On-Demand
(POD) system, where prints will never run out of
copies to be available for posterity.
The copyright owner is free to republish with other
publishers anytime.

KDP ISBN: 9798396082205
Independently Published

Contact: job_elizes@yahoo.com +
https://www.facebook.com/rafael.evangelista.5036459 +
http://tinyurl.com/mj76ccq (amazon site) +
www.tatayjoboelizes.webs.com +
https://www.facebook.com/groups/399368500835109

....

Author

About the author:

Rafael E. Evangelista is a retired capital partner of Baker McKenzie, the largest international law firm in the world.

This is the resume' of Rafael E. Evangelista –

Lawyer, banker, diplomat.
Co-founder, Task Force Good Governance;

Board member, Bank of Commerce (former vice-chairman and executive committee member);

Various memberships in corporate boards including the Rizal Chapter and the Makati branch of the Philippine National Red Cross;

Board chairman of the NOVA Foundation for the Less Abled;

National Commander, Defenders of Bataan and Corregidor;

and Honorary Consul of the Republic of Lithuania to the the Philippines.

Retired Capital Partner, Baker & Mckenzie (international law practice),
and Member, Board of Trustees, Ateneo de Manila
University.

Attended Ateneo de Manila University (A.B., Ll.B.),
Georgetown University (Master of Laws), with an honorary Ph.D. from St. Louis University. Recipient
of the Lithuanian Congressional Gold Medal of Honor.

....

Dedication

Dedication I would like to dedicate this first, and hopefully not last, compendium of essays and poetry written by me to the following:

1. My parents, **Dr. Rafael E Evangelista** and **Encarnacion E. Evangelista**. My father was a real life war hero and a medical doctor who healed at no cost to his patients. In many ways, he was my life's inspiration of "service to others." My mom was the first real writer in the family. It was she who first encouraged me to write at an early age.

2) My sister, **Rhona E. Centeno**, the other real writer in the family with my mom. She won multiple award for her literary writings. She graduated with two Summa Cum Laude degrees, both completed in four years.

3) **Father Joseph O'Hare S.J.** was my freshman professor in English. He was a pillar of encouragement

to my writing. He was the first person who insisted that I publish my works.

4) **Father Miguel Bernad S.J.** was the moderator of the Heights, the literary publication of the Ateneo. He caused the publication of some of my works to encourage me to share my writings with others.

I dedicate this book to these five persons who played such a singular role, each of them, in my literary life. Thank you.

....

Preface and Acknowledgment

Writing has been a passion of mine for almost as long as I can remember. I recall writing essays, short stories and poems as early as the age of 12 years.

Unfortunately, collecting and publishing whatever I had written never warranted the same attention I had given to writing them. Many, if not most of my articles and poems were lost over the years, with little recollection on my part of what, when, and where I wrote. Only a few were ever published.

Most of what I wrote had been scribbled on notebooks and left to fade on forgotten bookshelves. With the advent of computers and cellular phones, my writings were confined to the memory banks of these machines. As the machines turned obsolete, whatever writings were in them were simply confined to oblivion because I never transcribed what I had written.

Obviously, printing and publishing what I had written in the past did not occupy any position of priority in my mind's scheme of things.

I had been writing for many, many years simply for the joy of writing, and the joy of writing was for my self-fulfillment alone. I felt no need to share my thoughts, my dreams, my ambitions with anyone.

Or so I thought!

An old Jesuit professor of mine, Fr. Joseph O'Hare, S.J., who went on to become the President of Fordham University years later, was the first person to jiggle the notion that writing is only half the task of, well, writing! He told my parents at the end of my freshman year at the Ateneo de Manila University that their son was "intellectually selfish." He told them that I had refused to publish anything I had written, even in the school literary digests. The term he actually used to describe me was "intellectual bum."

Fr O'Hare complained to my parents that I had shown no interest in publishing, and hence in sharing, any of my writings. In so many words, he was telling my parents that while I had the talent to write, I was too selfish to share. Fr O'Hare's words did not sink in for many years.

A few years afterwards, another Jesuit professor, Fr. Miguel Bernad S.J., actually had some of my pieces published in the literary magazine of the Ateneo, The Heights, without my knowledge. As before, I had no interest in publishing what I wrote. And Fr. Bernad felt he had to take matters into his own hands.

Giving back was all this fuss was about. My two Jesuit professors and my parents were complicit in reminding me through the years that if someone had been given a gift, the gift was meant to be shared. Writing was only half of my life's mission of writing. Publishing and sharing with others completed the giving back required.

Although I have self published a number of Haiku poetry books over the past couple of years, this book "My Take 1" is the first comprehensive presentation of my writings - essays and poetry alike. For this effort, I have a new found friend, Jobo Elizes, from across the seas in the United States who encouraged me to publish this book, and beyond that, offered to publish the book himself.

I am grateful to my parents, Fathers O'Hare and Miguel Bernad S.J., and Jobo Elizes for all their encouragement that finally resulted in the publication of this book. I am likewise very grateful to have been afforded the opportunity of giving back and sharing with others, and hope my efforts are worth the reader's while. Rafael E Evangelista 12 May 2023

....

Contents

....

1
Sharing More Haikus With You

Colored Glasses

*Through the prism of
Colored glasses: softly,
Fall.
Then Winter, sharply.*

(REE, 6 January 2020)

Scorched

*The tear slowly falls,
The last of many that fell.
A scorched heart rages.*

(REE, 12 January 2020)

Shadows

Shadows race across
The grasslands, chasing after
Clouds that paint the sky.
(REE, 21 January 2020)

Heartbroken

I am heartbroken.
My soul may not remember
You, when I am gone.

(REE, 30 January 2020)

....

2
Searching Among Spring Rainbows

A breeze blows through my window.
In the shifting light of the evening star,
The silk curtains sigh and gently flow
To love's song floating from afar.

Is that you, my love, in the gentle light
Of evening, singing softly to me?
I reach out to touch and catch the sight
Of the star's soft rays I clearly see.

A night bird coos in the deep shadows
Of needle pines and late winter green,
Coaxing spring blooms to show and grow,
As now in darkness they sleep unseen.

The sky and the woods speak of love
Even as I miss you through the night.
I will search for you among stars above,

And love you with the coming light.

Wait for me wherever you might be.
I will search for you in early spring
Beyond the mountains and the sea
To hear the music of your love sing.

I know that you have waited for me
Through all these winter days gone,
Your smile once more I hope to see
Beneath spring rainbows of the sun.

(Raffy Evangelista 18 April 2021)

....

3
Federalism and Political Dynasties

Charter change to Federalism and while continuing to espouse Political Dynasties could be a perfect XXXosthu for national disaster. A dire forecast is that the government of each federal state could be controlled by political dynasties. With the National Government, and federal state governments, rotationally dominated by political dynasties, continuing control from the top of the power pyramid of government by select family groups can be assured.

Even now, after the recent national elections, and even without Federalism in place, more and more political dynasties have been elected into power. Federalism, with autonomous or semi autonomous states, sitting below the national government, can only exacerbate the situation of centralized control. Specially where the national government and the governments of each state form a cabal to consolidate and perpetuate themselves in power. It is not farfetched to autocratic or populist groups could, and would, utilize this lethal combination to perpetuate themselves in power.

If it happens, so much for the constitutional mandate that Sovereignty resides in the people, and all governmental authority emanates from them. This mandate will be trashed in all but words by those who would want to stay in control forever.

Look too to the repeal or radical amendment of the Local Government Code which gives flesh to the constitutional dictate that Sovereignty resides in the people. The LGC proclaims the barangay as the basic unit of government. Contrary to what is happening even today, nothing can, or should, happen in any barangay without the approval of the Barangay Assembly. The Assembly is the highest body in a Barangay, not the Barangay Chairman or his Barangay Council. It is noteworthy that the Barangay Assembly is comprised in membership by all residents of the barangay. Technically, the Assembly should not be under the dictates of city, provincial or national government above. This is Democracy at work, with the power flowing from bottom up.

Let us guard against the now revived move to create a federal government. And continue to fight to de-insitutionalize political dynasties once and for all!

Raffy Evangelista 13 May 2022

....

4
Roe v Wade

I have always been against abortion, and believe that life starts in the womb. I maintain that a baby need not be self sustaining in order to considered alive. Even a new born baby is incapable of sustaining itself either right after birth and for a period thereafter without its parents. This new born clearly has the right to life, and arbitrarily terminating that life is wrong. So too, in my humble opinion, with an unborn baby still in the womb.

Science has shown that life truly exists in the womb. Unborn babies learn and thrill at the sound of its mother's voice while in womb. They recognize external signals from the mother. They even move in the womb to music played to them. They can learn and unlearn things while still in the womb.

And who can forget those terrifying x-ray pictures of the unborn baby trying desperately to avoid the metal probes that had been inserted into its mother's womb to abort the baby's life? The unborn baby knows. The unborn baby thinks. The unborn baby feels. If it knows, if it thinks, if it feels, is it too much to conclude that the unborn child has a soul and the right to life?

What is difference between the umbilical cord that connects the baby to the mother in the womb, and the mother's breast that nurses the new born? Would I agree with a mother who refuses to give sustenance to a baby, born or unborn, on the basis of her alleged right of choice? Does she really have under these circumstances the right of choice not to nurse, and to starve, her new born to death?

I truly believe that the baby in either case has the primordial right to life. I believe the right to life of the baby takes precedence to any alleged right of choice of anyone …to terminate the life of the child!

There are concerns obviously about what happens to an unwanted child if its life is not terminated in the womb. A baby produced as a consequence of a rape, for example. I believe that is where the State and the Church should step in, by developing programs that will take full care and protection of the unwanted child, while protecting and helping the mother as well.

Roe v Wade seeks to protect the alleged right of choice of the mother with no regard for the right to life of the child, regardless of the circumstances of the conception of the child, whether rape, a drunken night out, or consensual sex. I think that is legally erroneous.

I am for the repeal of Roe v Wade. However, the jury, at least for me, is still out on the question of what to replace that decision with.

I tread on sensitive grounds with my stand. I risk offending both relatives and friends who have taken the opposite view. And I hurriedly stress that I merely am expressing my fundamental belief that:

The right to life of the child, whether born or still unborn, takes precedence to the right of choice of anyone to terminate the life of the child!

(REE, 25 March 2022)

....

5
The Smartmatic Fiasco

The simultaneous disruptive malfunctioning of the Smartmatic machines (supplied by allies of the current dispensation) in so many places seems too widespread to be coincidental. The fact that many of the official pollwatchers reportedly are also coming up with identical reactions expressed to the voters – "Leave your ballots with us. We will take care of submitting them" – seems like a scripted line to facilitate possible massive cheating in conjunction with the malfunctioning machines. Maybe NAMFREL and other watch dogs can start the investigative process going, starting with the Smartmatic machines. A cross section testing of affected machines across the country should be examined and scrutinized by independent technical investigators sponsored by Namfrel to see if this I was simply a case of simultaneous combustion or the result of some devious plan to cheat in these elections.

Raffy Evangelista May 9, 2022

....

6

Some of the things to watch out for at the voting precincts

1.Defective/malfunctioning voting machines. Per Comelec admission, there have been thus far over 2000 machines that have malfunctioned

2.Deletion from of voters voting list.

3.Pre filled ballots

4.Suggestion to leave ballots with Comelec officials

5.Adding to ballots names of candidates who were not voted for by the voter

6.Vote buying and ballot box snatching

7.Distribution within polling areas and precincts of sample ballots, some inserted with the real ballots in the official folder

8.Preying on Senior and PWD voters by poll watchers, usually by offering to help these voters in the filling up and casting of their ballots

9.Preshaded ballots

10.No official receipts shown/given to voter after voting, or dropping of the receipts in non official drop boxes

11. No marking of finger with indelible ink.

12.Distribution of defective, torn, or pre marked regular ballots. Even a simple ball pen dot can lead to the conclusion of a marked or soiled ballot. This is then accompanied with a refusal to replace the soiled ballot.

13. Destruction of regularly cast ballots

14.Power interruptions and breakdowns . There have been thus far a recorded 201 power interruptions from 4am to 11am of May 9, election day

This list is non-exclusive. Cheating can take place in many other ways.

Please be on guard.

Raffy Evangelista 9 May 2022

....

7

Tale of Courage and Commitment of Evelyn Nazareno

Many of us have seen the poignant and heart wrending picture of the 77 year old woman, bed ridden and connected to life sustaining medical tubes while in attendance at the Miting de Avance of Leni Pangilinan and Kiko Robredo. She insisted on attending the rally despite being ill with terminal cancer. She had a Leni for President tarp draped over the lower half of her body. Her name? EVELYN NAZARENO, a long time resident of La Vista Village and for many years an active XXXosthumousl of the Sta. Maria Della Strada Church on Katipunan Ave, QC.

I have known Evelyn for many years. I used to live in Loyola Heights Subdivision that sits almost directly in front of La Vista. We both belonged to the Della Strada Parish Community, where Evelyn was, for many years one of the Parish's most active members. Specially in projects involving and affecting the poor … always guided by the two Ignatian principles of "A Man For Others" and "For The Greater Glory of God." Simply put, for all the years I knew Evelyn she always sought to do God's will and to help others.

Which brings up the intriguing question about Evelyn. If she was, and is so sick, what was she doing at the Miting de Abance, at so much risk to herself and her already disease wracked body? Was she simply making a public display of herself to gain "brownie points" and admiration from the people at the rally? Was she rather a reckless person who simply wanted to self flagellate in public? Was she in such despair that her public act was of one who wants to commit suicide? Or was she simply drive to endorse the candidate for President of her choice?

I truly believe that the answer is: "None of the above!" Endorsing Leni as her candidate of choice is simply, I truly believe, merely a part of the answer – Evelyn felt compelled to express the message of her soul.

In the midst of her medical and physical woes, Evelyn decided to rise above all, and to cast her vote for God and Country.

God bless you always, dear friend!
(REE, October 2021)

....

8
Governance From The Top

A large segment of our population elected Du30 and continue to support him for now on the basis of the perception that he is a strong leader who promises change, a change they so desperately want. This is what I call a choice of governance based on leadership. The voters have chosen on the basis of their perception that this man is a strong leader who will bring about the change they want. Pretty much the same can be said of the protracted rule of Marcos, Sr.

The trouble with this system of governance is that strong leadership alone has led to populist, autocratic regimes (the regimes of Stalin, Hitler, Mao Tse Tung, Pol Pot, Marcos, to name a few) that have abused their centralized power, including favoring a few who believe and support these leaders. That is in fact how they remain in power- by supporting a few, eg. Army generals who in turn will assure the army's support for the leader.

Governance based on leadership alone seldom leads to the success of Lee Kwan Yu of Singapore. Lee, although he established a strong man rule in his country, was blessed to have a strong and informed citizenry behind him. The success of leadership by strong men is more the exception than the rule. The regimes of Hitler, Stalin, Mao Tse Tung, Pol Pot, Marcos ultimately failed for this reason – centralized power tends to be abused over time.

To succeed, a political system must have a broader base, what I call governance of good citizenship. An informed, involved, committed and dedicated citizenry – a true government of, for, and by the people – must be the true source of governance. And this must mean more than simply the power to vote. This means that the citizens must be empowered so that the power of governance flows from them and the communities they belong to (i.e., from their barangays) or ground up, rather than from Malacanang or top down. With this structure, good leadership could and should follow because governance based on a committed and informed citizenry will inevitably and eventually produce good and leaders.

Is this possible? The answer is that the current Constitution and existing laws already provide us with the opportunity to establish a governance of strong and informed citizens. It is a Constitution and system of laws where, if harnessed properly, power of governance flows from ground (the Barangay) up to Malacanang, and not the other XXXosthud. But many, if not most, of us are unaware, and have not been made aware (deliberately?) of the powers currently invested in the people by the current Constitution and implementing laws that could and would allow us now to have a government truly of the people, for the people, and by the people.

The fault does not lie with the current Constitution or with the people. The sad state of democratic affairs in our country is primarily due to the continued failure of our so called leaders to recognize and submit to the sovereignty of the people, and their adamant refusal to implement the basic tenets of governance provided for in the current Constitution. That was true of the Marcos regime, particularly during the Martial Law era. That is true of Du30's regime.

Thus, as an example, the Constiution provides that the highest political body at the grassroots, the Barangay, is the Barangay Assembly, comprised of the Barangay residents. Not the Barangay Chairman or the Barangay Council that he leads.

It is unfortunate even as we already have a Constitution that would focus the role of governance in the hands of the people, there are still people who support and would continue the current practice of governance from the top. Watch out for the candidates in the coming elections who would simply centralize the power of governance in Malacanang. We must head off these leaders off at the pass. (Raffy Evangelista, 11 December 2021)

....

9

True Leadership and Sovereignty

The best leadership is leadership by example. This type of leadership can mean to lead from up front. But just as often, it can mean the leader supporting the pack from the back. Many times, that kind of leadership means following and accepting the wishes of the people where the judgement of the people is sound. It means serving and following the sound judgement of the people. It means being a true Servant Leader of the people.

Sadly, we have seen only populist forms of governance with FEM and with Du30. The leader leads, and dictates, where the people should go. Since LBM's only real exposure to leadership is to the autocratic style of his father, and probably to Du30, what kind of leadership can we, should we, expect from LBM? Only more of the same.

We lost a golden opportunity for true servant leadership with Leni Robredo. Leni spontaneously joined the crowds who had decided to stay out under the rain at her rallies. By doing so, Leni was XXXosthumouslyXXX that in the final analysis it is the people who can, and should lead. So like a true Servant Leader, she stood with the people in the rain. And I believe that God blessed the gathering and her at that moment by stopping the rain!

Dear Lord, please bless the Filipino People with enlightened leadership henceforth. Bless us with true Servant Leaders who will know when to lead from the front and from the back, but always in accordance with the wishes of the people. Bless us with leaders who have the humility and wisdom to understand that the collective wisdom and judgement of the people should always be accorded primacy in matters of governance, and that the people are the true Sovereign!

(Raffy Evangelista, 1 May 2022)

....

10
To all populists –

Crossing The Line

You crossed the Line!

You violated the Line!
You stomped on the Line!
You erased the Line!
And now our country's
Time is running out,
You hope that the
Line Will save you?
How dare you!
Lives have been lost!
Love has been lost!
Trust and credibility
Have been lost!
Democracy was Lost before.
The Nation has been
Brought to danger!
The Nation could
Have been lost,
Because you deformed
That sacred Line
And manipulated it
As your own, and
For your own ends!
We are the People!
We own that Line!
And yet you tried to
Take it from us and
Abuse it as your own!
You taught your own
To believe that we do
Not own or deserve
That sacred Line!
You taught your own to
Rant and rave against us
When it was really you
Who tried to steal
The blessed Line!
How dare you!
How dare you!
How dare you!

We, the People, will
Reclaim the Line!
Sovereignty resides
In the People, and
All government authority
Emanates from them.
The Sovereign
Line is ours!
We are the coming Storm!
We are the People!
We are Sovereign,
Even amidst
The maelstrom!

(REE, 8 January 2021)

....

11
Spread The Truth!

The spread of communism and authoritarianism starts when people are silenced. Free speech is the first freedom citizens lose.

The best way we know to combat this is to continue to fight for the Truth and the right to spread it.

And Democracy needs your help. Historical revisionism and the distortion, and even the denial, of the truth are ongoing even now. It will only accelerate as we move closer to future elections. Let us all make a stand for the truth NOW!

Make A Stand Now

Death of the sinagtala,
Death of the fireflies in the skies
Death of the rainbows

Death of the wind's gentle sighs.

What happened to our world before
When wrong people came to power,
Can happen again if we fail to fight!
Our children, their families will suffer!

Some feign ignorance and disaffection.
How can they sit back and not dare?
Our heroes died in the field of sacrifice.
Not simply fearful, some just don't care!

On our land, the sun will either rise or set.
What is it that we wish to preside over?
If we do not now have the backbone,
Our Country could be lost forever.

The sun disappeared from sight before.
Shall we let darkness set on us again?
But that is what our Country is facing
Unless we make a stand now, not then.

We dream of stars shining in our skies,
Of the sun again lighting up our day.
Let us stand strong together as one
And let God's bidding guide our way.

"Para sa Diyos at Bayan," our cry,
In glorious battle and blessed peace.
Bring back the sinagtala and rainbows.
Love for Country must never cease.

(Raffy Evangelista, 14 April 2022)

12

Leni, Kiko And Beyond

"Can you hear the people sing,
Singing the song of angry men?
It is the music of the people
Who will not be slaves again!"

One of the most powerful lines
Of any song ever written to
Express the innate desire of
Men to be free and sovereign!
Today, as we fight for
Full Sovereignty and Democracy,
We can foresee people's
Rallies along the way, and
The raising of voices in unison:

"When the beating of your heart
Echoes the beating of the drums
There is a life about to start
When tomorrow comes!"

The new dawn is coming,
Tomorrow is on its way.
The light will erase the dark.
Let enlightened leaders lead the way.

"Di n'yo ba naririnig?
Tinig ng bayan XXXosthumo
Himig ito ng Pilipinong
Di muli palulupig."

"Ikaw ba'y makikibaka
at hindi maduduwag
Na gisingin ang mga
panatikong bingi't bulag,
Kasinungalingan labanan
hanggang mabuwag?"

*"Do you hear the people sing
Singing the song of angry men?
It is our music that they sing:
We will not be slaves again!"*

*Fight, fellow countrymen!
Bring the fight to
Today And Beyond!*

(Raffy Evangelista, 18 March 2022)

....

13
A Message from the Lord –

*I AM WHO AM:
I AM JESUS.
I AM YOUR NEW LIFE.*

*I AM this very MOMENT.
I AM today,
I am this YEAR.
I AM your PAST,
I am your FUTURE.
I AM the FRESH PAGE
in your book of time.
I AM the WISDOM to make sense
of all failures and sorrows.
I AM the FOUNT of all
joy and happiness.
All the BLESSINGS
that you sought and
did not find are in the
Palm of My Hand,
All the GOOD that you*

tried to do but did not achieve,
All that you DREAMED
for but did not get,
All that you HOPED for but
did not have the will to strive for,
All the FAITH that you claimed
but did not fulfill,
I AM the POWER to
make them all come true.
I AM the WORD.
I AM the EUCHARIST.
I AM LOVE.
I AM the ONE who makes
all things new.
I AM your MAKER.
I AM your REPAIRER.
I AM your HEALER.
I AM your RESTORER.
I Am your SAVIOR.
I AM JESUS,
your NEW DAY.
I AM JESUS,
your NEW LIFE.
I AM JESUS,
your NEW YEAR.
COME AND YOUR NEW LIFE
WILL BE BLESSED BY ME!

(Raffy Evangelista, 1 Feb 2022)

....

14
Do Not Weep For Me

I wrote this poem on the passing year ago of a dear friend, **Vicente Diego Locsin.** The theme of the poem is that Diego is not gone. He merely sleeps. Diego is the one who speaks in the poem. –

Do Not Weep For Me

My family and friends went to a
Funeral of someone dear today,
The whispers could be heard
As the mourners turned to pray.

There was deep sadness as
The Minister blessed the dead.
I watched and saw my loved ones
With abundant tears to shed.

I felt words forming in my heart:
"No tears for me, your beloved one,
I merely sleep as darkness sets,
To rise again with the coming sun."

Perhaps I conveyed some calm
To those who gathered briefly.
I felt some peace among them,
As they bowed to pray quietly.

Soon there was silence, as I was
Left with God and His Love to keep.
So I then waited for the sun to rise
Even as I closed my eyes to sleep.

(Raffy Evangelista, 30 January 2022)

....

15
Sharing something cultural –

JITNEYS

I received this email from my sister who lives in California –

"I was watching the New Year Pasadena Rose Bowl Parade, & as a jitney made its way, the announcer said the name for the vehicle came from the five cent fare to ride it. He said jitney means five cents. Did you know that?"

This was my response to my sister –

The word "jitney" is a Filipino contraction of the name "Jeep." After WW II, there were almost no motorized vehicles left on the road except American Army jeeps and trucks. Given Filipino resourcefulness, jeeps were converted to public utility vehicles which Filipinos called "Jeepneys," which name was subsequently contracted to "Jitneys."

The word "Jeep" is a brand name of the car manufacturer Willy's. There was another near identical vehicle of similar use during WW II produced by Ford Motors. For some obscure reason, both the Willy's and Ford products came to be commonly referred to as "Jeeps."

Originally, fare on these converted jeeps or jitneys was 10 centavos, and shortly after 20 centavos. The rate of exchange then was 10 centavos = five cents. In 1962, the Philippine currency underwent a devaluation. 20 centavos became the standard rate for jitney fare. At that time the rate of exchange was 20 centavos = five cents. That is where this story you narrate of 5 cents probably stems from.

The jitney as a means of local public transportation became institutionalized. Jitney manufacturers like Sarao started producing vehicles garnished with paintings, portraits, and the like, making jitneys one of a kind in the world. Some are real works of art. Jitneys became ingrained into Philippine culture.

Of course, jitneys are no longer made from WW II jeeps. They are now converted mostly from Toyota, Nissan and other popular Japanese brands. I find it ironic that Filipinos are now riding around in vehicles with Japanese made motors after WW II, and have embraced these vehicles made by their former enemies as their own.

There has been a move to phase out jitneys from Philippine roads as non efficient means of transportation. But the resistance has been strong. Part of the resistance is for economic reasons, ie, jitneys provide a means of XXXosthumous for the jitney drivers. But the cultural factor is also very intense. Many feel that the streets of the Philippines will never be the same without the jitney.

Raffy Evangelista 3 January 2022

....

16
A Call For Change In Mindset

Filipinos must start condemning the "petty, personal attacks" that have become rife in Philippine politics. They must call on government officials, starting with President Duterte, to follow the examples of our great Filipino Statesmen of yesteryears who raised and debated issues, rather than personalities: Presidents Quezon, Osmena, Senators Recto and Diokno, among others.

The season of divisiveness in the country has become so deep that it is critical that we reject what has become far too common in our country: name calling, petty personal attacks, doing and saying whatever it takes just stay in power or to get one's way in politics.

It is dangerous to continue to do so, specially when we are exposed not just internal, but more specially to external threats, the likes of which the Philippines has not seen since Imperial Japan tried to impose on Southeast Asia it's much proclaimed "Japanese Co-Prosperity Sphere." The Belt-Road program of China and its 9 Yard Dash Line in the South China Sea clearly proclaims China's intention to take over Southeast Asia and beyond, darkly echoing what Imperial Japan tried to do 80 years ago.

To continue to be so divided as a people not only lessens who we are as a country, but also stops us from recognizing fully as one nation the kind of threat China poses for the Philippines today.

There must be a better way forward. We can work with people who are different from us. We can be friends with people who are different from us. We can love and care about people who are different than us. We can keep people who are different than us safe. We can be good people who care deeply about each other even when we disagree.

We can start by listening to someone with a different opinion—listening not to rebut or debate, but listening to understand. We can articulate our own opinions and beliefs without believing or saying that someone else's are, therefore, wrong. We can embrace difference while seeking common ground.

Trolling one another, fighting one another on social media or any other kind of media is simply not the answer.

We must all agree to "double down" on such an inclusive approach, vowing to represent the Filipino people "not by calling names or playing political games, but by showing up and doing the work to keep Philippines moving forward."

We must all reflect on the legacy left behind by our hero statesmen who dedicated their lives for a united and greater Philippines, among them our martyrs Josefa Escoda, Jose Abad Santos and Vicente Lim. Trolling and fighting one another diminishes Filipinos as a people and the Philippines as a country.

Unity may be the only way we can survive the double whammy of external and internal threats like China and political misfits pose for the Philippines.

(REE, 20 December 2021)

....

17
Joseph Hunt Francia

In every community, in every group, in every class, there are those types who go about their daily lives with a certain amount certain of "humbug," the daily calibration of rituals that some persons go through to push for and maintain a position and place in "respectable" society.

There are those who fall into the "withdrawn" category, the victims of insecurities, born from physical or emotional shortcomings, real or imagined, and have otherwise had difficult lives. Sadly, society has also not always been kind and XXXosthumouslyXXX to those who are perceived to fall short of accepted communal standards of physicality and intellect.

Then there are also those who are gifted intellectually and otherwise, but who see no need to blow their own trumpets because they are totally secure in their God-given gifts, persons who feel no desire to parade themselves on life's catwalk, just to gain the respect or adulation of others.

To my mind, Joseph definitely belonged to this third and last group. Surely, like all of us, Joseph must have had his hurts and disappointments in life, but he never was a sorry victim of self or of society. Joseph had his share of gifts – his keen intellect, his easy smile, and his lively sense of humor that sometimes boarded on the corny. He was one of the more intellectually gifted members of our school batch, and a consistent honor student. He had a wonderful singing voice. Graduating college with one of those Latin honors that seemed so remote to ordinary students like me, clearly Joseph was no intellectual slouch. He was the kind of student who seemed to be able to get good marks in much the same easy way that he could, and would, flash his ever present smile, with a minimum of trying .

But despite these gifts, Joseph was never one to brag or trumpet his accomplishments. And in that sense he was always one of the most humble members of our class. Not too many of us are aware that he devoted most of his adult life to social work, as a student, then as a priest, and finally as a layman. As a another good friend observed, "I never realized how many social outreach programs Bobby was involved in until people wrote about his involvements in Face Book after he passed away."

Joseph cared, and cared immensely, for others. For a good number of years, I had been tasked to inform classmates/batchmates of developments affecting the class or individual classmates. Joseph always responded with a txt or a call to inquire what he could do, how the classmate or his family was doing, and always with an offer of a prayer.

School, specially in Grade School and High School, is often marked by the exhuberance of youth. Sometimes this translates into the excessive and the negative: bullying and fights, certainly arguments and bickering. Most of us have been involved in some or more arguments and bickering during our student days. One of the most surprising conclusions I had to make about Joseph, even as I mulled over this talk about him, was that I could not remember a single instance where he had a fight or argument with a classmate. As surprisingly, I could not remember any instance when Joseph was ever disagreeable with any one.

Which is not to say Joseph would or could never disagree. But as always, in his own firm way, he had a way of telling others, me included, of his own different point of view, without being offensive.

I think Joseph firmly believed in the old adage: it is ok to disagree as long as you are not disagreeable. I envied those who had that gift, because quite frankly I did not always succeed in the practical application of that principle. Joseph epitomized the ability to press a point without ever being truly disagreeable. Exasperating sometimes certainly, but never disagreeable.

Joseph decided somewhere along the way to live a simple and humble life, a life centered on his firm belief and commitment to social justice. The times Joseph and I would bump into each other, he would talk with great enthusiasm and exhuberance about the social programs and projects he was involved in. Sadly, the last time I had such a conversation with him was in a phone call the day before he died. Typically, he did not speak about about himself. We talked that afternoon about a topic of common interest to us: an interfaith project to push for barangay empowerment as the corner stone of our democracy.

Simple joys for a simple, humble, caring man: no flashy cars or clothes. No trappings of wealth or power. The man was definitely not a narcissist. It was all about others, and service to and for those others. Joseph was one of those Ateneans who truly epitomized the classic reference to St Thomas More: a Man for Others. That was what Joseph was all about.

Good night, Joseph, we bid you farewell, even as you travel to the Light beyond the bend. Please share with the Good Lord some of those patented smiles of yours for us as you enter His embrace. Good night, dear friend, good night!

(REE, 20 November 2019)

....

18
Not Political

Hey you guys? You know how a lot of you say you just aren't "political"?

This is a real photo of some of the staff at Auschwitz on a break.

This photo was taken AT Auschwitz, WHILE they worked there. Not before the Holocaust, and certainly not after. DURING. These actual people are on a break from working in Auschwitz.

Look at them. Honestly, take 30 seconds of your time and look at their faces.

They "weren't political."

They never thought of themselves as evil. It was where and when they were born that put them in 1930s Germany. They were not inherently evil people at all, to begin with or ever. Because it doesn't take natural born monsters. It doesn't take the one in a million kind of person who enjoys murder, who you can tell from a mile away is a bad egg.

It's the perfectly nice, normal person trying to go about daily life without "being political." The ones who go with the flow. Who don't raise a fuss, or step out of line.

These are the faces of people who "aren't political."

And somewhere in their immediate vicinity, maybe at the exact moment this photo was being taken, Anne Frank's mother was being starved to death.

So please. Don't kid yourselves. Look around you at what's happening in our country. We have people of a similar mold or frame of mind.

These persons in the picture are people who saluted the racist speeches of their leader, who ignored the murders he undertook in the name of his Mein

Kampf. Here, there are those who laugh at crude and insulting jokes against women. Who laugh when their mysoginistic uncle talks about having commuted murder and rape. Who applaud when that uncle insults God and religion, and says his god is Satan. Who just want to coo over people's babies and dogs on social media and get annoyed when the conversation turns to current affairs and human rights. Who know they should vote in coming elections but, ugh, hate getting up early to do so.

Don't kid yourselves. That's exactly who these people are. And if at this moment in time you yourself are "not political," know that the rest of us know exactly what that means.

You're one of them. (REE, 22 January 2022)

....

19
Gago, Jokes And The Four Way Test, The Worst Joker Leader We Have Ever Had –

The sun has set on Duterte's administration. Thank God!

One of the damning legacies of his administration is its distortion and total disregard of the truth.

We have been told by the man himself that we are gago if we believe! But then he also said we gago if we do not believe. Are we to be damned if we do, and damned if we don't?

"How can the person's word be trusted on anything? He has made so many declarations on matters of serious concerns and later claims what he declared are merely "jokes!" How can he pretend to be a leader if everything he says is, or can be turned into, a joke? His worst "jokes" are lewd or grotesque or simply in bad taste. How can such jokes be the mark of a true leader? How are we to react, what are we to do, when his off color jokes are so bad that they do not qualify as jokes at all, despite any claims to the contrary?

The XXXosthumnary defines the noun "joke" as: "a thing that someone says to cause amusement or laughter, especially a story with a funny punch line," and as a verb as: "talking humorously or flippantly." Clearly from these definitions, lewd and grotesque jokes do not qualify as true jokes. More accurately, they are non-jokes since they lack humor and are not funny.

Why then do people laugh and applaud at non-jokes of this man?

The "joke" of this man about sticking his fingers into the private parts of a sleeping woman fails the funny and humorous test miserably. My parents and grandparents would have been mortified by this so called joke. My elders always taught me not to entertain this type of non-jokes, including so called green jokes, because they are really insults told at the expense of others, mostly women."

Now when this man calls for the religious leaders, or anyone else for that matter, to be killed, how can any one in his right mind call that a joke? This "killer joke" goes far, far beyond green jokes, and even the "joke" about molesting a sleeping woman. This is a "joke" about murder, plain and simple. People in their right minds do not make jokes about killing others! But perhaps that is precisely the real question to be in this exercise: Was the man in his "right mind?"

Now, what this should make of his rabid followers and the fence sitters who laugh at the "jokes" about the sexual molestation of the sleeping woman or the killing of religious leaders? I wonder whether they would still have laughed if the man turned to them one day and said, "I will kill you, or you should be killed." Could his band of merry men still have managed to laugh at this "joke" directed at them without some trepidation that the man may in fact mean it? Tough call. Can you still laugh with someone who says you should be killed, joke or no joke. But his followers laughed when this man said that religious leaders should be killed! We have to ask the same question of his followers. Are these followers in their "right mind?" Obviously, this is a case of "birds of the same feathers flocking together, all sharing a dark, dicey side with him who they adulate!

There is a more serious mind problem related to the proclivity of this man to make jokes. If we are to follow his lead, we must know when he was serious or not, and we must be able to determine what his intentions are. His position of the responsibility bore with it the gravitas of the highest office in the Land. We had a right to know when he was joking or not. It does not help anyone, specially the man himself, if we are called "gago" whenever we happen believe the "truths" that he proclaims. A practical consequence of being called gago often enough for believing what the man says is that we may simply tune out and stop believing. Where does that leave the man, the office of responsibility he held, and the gravitas it represented? Who then would have led, who then would have followed, if the people are left confused and discombobulated by this man's jokes?

The equation Is simple. We need to know the truth. Leadership means precisely that: TO LEAD! NOT TO MISLEAD! If the people never knew whether the Man was joking or not, they were being misled away from the truth. The inevitable consequence, simply put, was a failure of leadership. "Truth, and what and when it is the truth" had become the main issue for many Filipinos in those days. Truth has become so opaque because of the manipulation of what was and what wasn't. Would it have been fair to ask this leadership, "Are you coming or going?" "Where are you taking us? Where are you leading us?" "Lead, for heaven's sake! Enough of jokes already!"

Rotary International has set the bar with their 4 Way Test that the man would do well to have observed: 1) Is it the truth? 2) Is it fair to all concerned? 3) Will it build good will and better friendships? 4) Will it be beneficial to all concerned? Sadly, many of the things this man said were not the truth. By his own admission, they were mere jokes. Neither were his so called jokes fair: jokes about sexual molestation of a woman and killing of others can never be fair. Nor can jokes about sexual molestation or killing build good will and better friendships. And how such jokes can be beneficial to those who are victims of molestation or to those threatened with being killed is beyond comprehension.

The man had much to learn from the 4 Way Test for the truth!

(REE, 6 February 2022)

....

20
Love's Sunlight

Wake me up inside,
I feel the stirrings outside.
I know the gifts the mornings sing
And all the joy that they can bring.

But inside me night shadows
Still pace as rainbows prance
Outside in colors of the sun,
Awake before the night is done.

Where are the shining stars,
To tell me where you are?
In the darkness of my room
I search the shifting gloom.

Then I feel fingers of the sun
Warming the cold, fled and gone.
I blink to make the waking slow
And feel warmth just softly grow.

Love's light is what makes life
Worth struggling through strife,
Worth living through darkness.
Love blots out the sadness.

I shall win love's sunlight
By fighting for what is right
Beyond the distant gate,
Never for what I hate.

(Raf Evangelista, 24 May 2023)

....

21
You Walked Into My Life

I walked into your life
When I was not searching.
When I fell in love with you,
You were taking a chance
By letting me walk into your life,
And letting me love you.
You never asked me
About my past, and were
Willing to give me the chance
To fall in love once again.
You never asked even if
You had the right to do so.
I walked into your life
When I was lost, and then
I fell in love with you.
I never thought I would
Find anybody else.
It had been so long.
But then I fell in love again

When you softly smiled,
And very gently said, hello.
I walked into your life.
You took a chance with me.
When I was searching.
You gave me the chance
To fall in love once again,
To fall in love … with you.
I will never let you go.
I fell in love with you
When I was not wanting.
I walked into your life,
And I fell in love with you!
I still do!

(REE, 22 June 2022)

22
A Mother's Lament For Her Fur Baby Of Gold:

Chelsea

Days have gone by
Since you said goodbye,
My beautiful girl of gold.
Even when I am old,
I will remember you …
And how your love was true.

You would run to me,
Ignoring others when I'd be
Walking through the door.
So much of you to love, and more.
Your love unadulterated, pure,
Was there for all to see.
You wanted to make sure
I knew you truly loved me.

I miss you now that you are gone.
But I feel love from beyond the sun.
Is that where you wait for me?
Will you rush to me when you see
Me coming through Heaven's door,
As you did so many times before?
My girl of gold.
You will forever be
My golden fur baby,
Chelsea!

Mama Lou

(Raf Evangelista 24 March 2023)

23
Love's Slipstreams

Romance the soul,
Nurture the heart, and fly
Across the sky's slipstreams
That take all breath away.

Hear the patter of raindrops, the
Gently tapping at window panes
By our souls to wash away all hurts
And pain that might have been.

Touch and feel the sun and rain …
Sunshine and showers that
That paint flowers to bloom, and
So too that grow parched hearts.

Happiness, peace come both
With warmth, sunshine … even rain.
Dance, glide through gentle showers,
And feel the joy and calm they bring.

Through rain and sunshine,
I will hold you in tight embrace.
Have you ever felt the sunshine?
Have you ever listened to the rain?

Can I do otherwise but love you
Through the music of raindrops
And the waltz of soft sunlight that
Mesmerize my soul and my being?

I love you, my darling, and yes,
I sing to you through the seasons,
And fly in their slipstreams as
They glide gently into our hearts.
You will never be too near,
You will never be too far.
You will always be in the
Slipstreams of my heart.

Like blossoms that never leave
My garden, you will always
Be in my heart through
Winter, spring, summer or fall.

Fly languidly on your dreams
With your wings. I will join you
And fly and soar to the skies
And heaven above to see God.

He waits for you on high!

(REE, 19 October 2022)

....

24

Romeo Taruc and Nini Quezon Avancena – A Story of a Closure

Luis M Taruc

The Hukbong Bayan Laban sa Hapon, better known by its abbreviation Hukbalahap, was a socialist guerrilla movement formed by the farmers of Central Luzon. It's founder was Luis Taruc and operated from 1942 to 1954, mainly in Central Luzon. The Hukbalahap movement was one of the most effective fighting forces during the Philippine resistance against Japan during World War II.

Luis Mangalus Taruc (1913 – 2005) a Filipino hero of the resistance against Japan during WW II, was the leader of the Hukbalahaps until 1950. His involvement with the agrarian movement came when as a student he was initiated into the problems of the farmers.

An avowed socialist, Luis Taruc was General Secretary of the Socialist Party of the Philippines. In 1938, the Partido Socialista (Socialist Party) formed a United Front with the ("teamed up" but maintained its separate identity. Taruc himself maintained that his group were not communists)with the Partido Komunista ng Pilipinas as part of the Common Front strategy, and Taruc assumed the role of Commander-in-Chief of the military wing of the United Front created to fight the Japanese.

At the height of its popularity, the Hukbalahap reached a fighting strength estimated at between 10,000 and 30,000. In 2017, the National Historical Commission of the Philippines declared Taruc a hero for being a "nationalist and defender of the rights of farmers and workers".

After the war against Japan, the Hukbalahap continued their demands for agrarian reform. Taruc and seven colleagues were elected to the House of Representatives but the government of Manuel Roxas did not allow them to take their seats in Congress. In the next five years, Taruc would give up on the parliamentary struggle and once more take up arms, this time against the new Republic.

In 1967, Taruc wrote He Who Rides the Tiger (1967). In it, he wrote " I know from experience, that the nationalism of the Communists is indeed opportunism, and that they use it for their own ends. Any nationalist who makes an ally of the Communist is going for a ride on a tiger."[1]:21 Additionally, Luis wrote, "For ruthlessness and cruelty are alien to Christian thought, and when men in the Free World use such methods, they do so in defiance of their own morality and ideals. The atheist Communist, however, believes that the end justifies the means, or in Lenin's words, 'Morality is subordinate to the class struggle.' For this reason, the Communist can pursue a policy of terror and cruelty with a clear conscience." In 2003, Taruc explained that he attributed the United Front's revolution's failure to the dogmatism of the Communist members of the politburo's Russian-trained elite, in particular brothers, Jose and Jesus Lava.

In June 1935, he married Feliciana Bernabe, and his sole offspring, his son Romeo was born in March 1936. Romeo later became a medical doctor and a staunch defender of the claim that his father, Luis, and a majority of the Hukbalahap Movement were not Communists, but Socialists fighting for social and agrarian reforms for the farmers and the poor.

Aurora Antonia Quezon

Aurora Antonia Quezon (February 19, 1888 – April 28, 1949) was the wife of Philippine President Manuel Luis Quezon and the First Lady of the Philippines from 1935 to 1944. Much beloved by Filipinos, Quezon was known for involvement with humanitarian activities and served as the first chairperson of the Philippine National Red Cross.

Mrs Quezon was killed in an ambush by Huk rebels on April 28, 1949 at the age of 61 years of age. In the ambush, Mrs Quezon also lost her elder daughter, Baby, and son in law, Felipe Buencamino, the first husband of her second daughter, Nini.

The ambush took place in what was then Baler, Tayabas. It has been renamed to Baler, Aurora to honor Mrs Quezon. Mrs Quezon was enroute to inaugurate a hospital dedicated to her late husband, President Manuel L Quezon who passed away in 1944.

Mrs Quezon had been cautioned about this trip beforehand due to the frequent insurgency activities in Central Luzon of the United Front of the Communist Party of the Philippines. She shrugged off the threat, remarking with self assurance on the morning of the trip, "[Hukbalahap Supremo] Taruc knows my white hair and he will not hurt me."

It was widely believed at the time of the assassination that the Huks, without distinction, were responsible for the killings. This belief was attributed without regard to which side of the so called United Front the attackers belonged to. Luis Taruc, supremo of the Hukbalahap, denied that his group was responsible for the crime, a denial he maintained until his death. He stated that the group he led as part of the United Front and were Socialists, not Communists. Most, he said, were simply farmers, non ideologues, seeking social justice and agrarian reform. He maintained it was the Lava brothers who were Communists and led the Communist side of the United Front.

Zeneida Quezon Avancena (Tita Nini)

"Most of Tita Nini's 100 years were as a family woman and staunch ally of justice and human rights. She always carried her family's legacy with grace and added her own pursuits befitting the needs of the time,"

Sen. Kiko Pangilinan said in a statement. Pangilinan praised her for her contributions during Martial Law.

"She lent her name and gravitas to difficult valuable causes, including those of political detainees. She made such an impact. After the Marcos dictatorship was toppled, she became a member of the Presidential Human Rights Committee, together with Senators Ka Pepe Diokno and Lorenzo Tañada," he recalled.

Former presidential spokesperson Edwin Lacierda meanwhile said "a light has dimmed once more, the country orphaned by her passing. A pillar of strength during the dark days of martial law. She never wavered when the country needed a voice & spoke by marching with the youth, despite her age," he said in a tweet.

Tita Nini lost her first husband, Felipe Buencamino, her mother, Mrs Aurora Quezon, and her sister, Baby, in the fatal ambush in Baler in 1949.

In 1951, she married her second husband, Alberto Avanceña.

Since then, she has been involved in human rights and social justice causes, even marching in her sixties in the Anti Marcos rallies that eventually led to the downfall of the Dictator.

Dr Romeo Taruc

Doctor Romeo Taruc, who passed away a few years ago when he was 84 years old, is the only son of Luis Taruc. Here are the insights recently shared by him:

Romeo's mother–Luis Taruc's wife–died when the younger Taruc was only two years old. Since then, he lived together with his relatives. Whenever people back then ask him regarding the whereabouts of his father, he would reply, "Nagpapapalaganap po (He's propagating)."

As a family of revolutionaries, it was accepted that life was not safe. More time was allotted to the cause of Philippine liberation and, mainly, land reform than one's own interests. Nevertheless, there was a year when both

Tarucs lived together in a mountain together with other Huks.

On April 28, 1949, it was reported that the First Lady of then President Manuel Quezon was shot dead together with other civilians in Nueva Ecija. Although there were other suspects accused of the ambush and Luis Taruc denied the next day the Huks' participation in the said tragedy, Doctor Romeo Taruc admitted that it was a mistake.

Dr Romeo Taruc stated in an interview,

"I already clarified with Nini Quezon–the last surviving daughter of late President Manuel Quezon–that it was not our intention to kill her mother. She was an unfortunate collateral damage."

The Huks–as they are also referred–fought together with American troops in ousting–through military and guerilla force–the Japanese invaders in the Philippines back in World War II.

Although it is known that they are not pro-American, they were willing to collaborate with American forces to help liberate the country from what seemed to be a more blatantly brutal foe back then. The Huks were more effective in certain operations than trained Filipino and American soldiers. For example, the late historian Teodoro Agoncillo wrote that when the Americans landed in Lingayen in January 1945, the Huks "already cleared out the Japanese obstacles.[2]"

Here are the insights shared by Dr Taruc-

6. 6 months to 1 year – the longest time together. Romeo's mother–Luis Taruc's wife–died when the younger Taruc was only two years old. Since then, he lived together with his relatives. Whenever people back then ask him regarding the whereabouts of his father, he would reply, "Nagpapalaganap po (He's propagating)."

As a family of revolutionaries, it was accepted that life was not safe. More time was allotted to the cause of

Philippine liberation and, mainly, land reform than one's own interests. Nevertheless, there was a year when both Tarucs lived together in a mountain together with other Huks. During our interview he initially said it was around 6 months, then later qualified that it may have been up to a year.

2. No special treatment. During the longest season both Tarucs were living together, one guerilla leader gave Romeo a nice leather belt. He recalled how his father rebuked that guerilla leader for giving Romeo a special treatment. His father believed that if they had to struggle together, then they had to maintain an atmosphere of impartiality. There were other guerrilla members and peasants suffering with them.

3. The ambush of Mrs. Quezon. On April 28, 1949, it was reported that the First Lady of then President Manuel Quezon was shot dead together with other civilians in Nueva Ecija. Although there were other suspects accused of the ambush and Luis Taruc initially denied the next day the Huks' participation in the said tragedy. Doctor Romeo Taruc admitted that it was a mistake.

The Huks were used to the usual set up that the First Lady did not have any grand military escort when she roams around. Therefore, when they saw that there were military officers riding through Nueva Ecija, they merely wanted to take their weapons from those officers until it resulted to shooting each other. They did not expect that Mrs. Quezon was inside one of the vehicles.

"I already clarified with Nini Quezon–the last surviving daughter of late President Manuel Quezon–that it was not our intention to kill her mother," explained Romeo. "She was an unfortunate collateral damage."

4. During Marcos' regime. The late President Ferdinand Marcos granted the release of Luis Taruc from prison[3] and became an "assembly man" to Marcos' parliament. In spite of this, the old Taruc continued the struggle for land reform.

The Taruc family, ling other guerrilla fighters, were thankful that the late President Marcos because he "lobbied for the benefits of Filipino war veterans in a special legislation called the G.I. Bill of Rights.[4]" The term "Filipino war veterans" included both the military and recognized guerrilla fighters[5]–including the Huks– who fought against the Japanese occupation during World War II.

Luis Taruc seemed to have been judged as a guerilla leader who "surrendered to the Marcos puppet regime" to the dismay of the leaders of the Communist Party of the Philippines, particularly Jose Ma. Sison.[6] The Huks reorganized after the war and merged together with the New People's Army at some point, but sometime during the 1950s or 1960s the leaders of the Huks–operating with a different name during the Post World War II Era–separated from the New People's Army although some members of both groups continued to participate together liberation activities, especially land reform.

It must be noted that even before the Japanese came, Luis Taruc was an active member of the Socialist Party–different from the Communist Party of the Philippines , though they would agree in the pursuit of some reforms, are linked by ideology, and later merged– who was advocating farmers, laborers, and peasants.[7]

The Huks–operating now with the name Hukbong Mapaglaya ng Bayan[8] or the People's Liberation Army–was different from the New People's Army because although both agreed at some point to overthrow the government[9] and use armed weapons in the process, Doctor Romeo Taruc said that his father– Luis Taruc–later solidified his position to achieve reforms through parliamentary process.

But did Luis Taruc become a traitor during the Marcos' regime against other communist-inspired movements?

"Tatay ko nuon nasa Manila, assembly man ni Marcos (My father was in Manila, Marcos' assembly man," Doctor Romeo Taruc recalls. "Ako nandito sa Central Luzon, kasama ng mga N.P.A. (I was here at Central Luzon, part of the New People's Army)."

They never gave up their struggle for the reforms they wanted to achieve.

5. Why Romeo became a medical doctor. Doctor Romeo Taruc works at 3G Medical Clinic and Laboratory at Balibago along MacArthur Highway, Angeles, Pampanga.

Frankly, this was not something the researcher would expect as a profession for a son of a revolutionary icon. Probably a businessman, politician, or some sort of mogul or statesperson but not a doctor.

Doctor Romeo Taruc explained that he was also part of his father's Huk movement. He was one of those taking care and nursing the sick and wounded guerilla fighters. He developed his knowledge through experience and formal education over time.

6. Other advocacy today. As a doctor, Sir Romy is concerned about prevalent health issues today. He is concerned about the spread of STD, HIV, and AIDS. He gives free consultation and counselling. His clinic's other professional services include Blood exams for HIV, Syphillis, Hepatitis B and Drug Test, cautery of warts, free medicines for STD (for clubs enrolled with 3G Clinic), mobile visits for clubs enrolled with 3G Clinic, papsmear, vaccination against cervical cancer.

Raffy Evangelista 2022

....

25
Haikus:

The Tears Are Gone

God painted my heart

With colors of happiness
That bring out my smiles.
REE, 12 February 2023

Specks?

Specks in the Cosmos of God,
Clinging to
His Hand!
REE, 13 February 2023

The Truth?

You alter the facts
To fit what you believe in!
Where then is God's truth?
REE, 14 February 2023

Renewal

True love does not stop
Just because of the sunset.
Sunrise brings new life!
REE, 15 February 2023

Be Worthy

Be worthy of love,
Be in love for a lifetime.
Any less is a waste.
REE, 16 February 2023

Guiding Hand

In the rush of day,
Fall back on love and believe.
A Hand guides the way.
REE, 17 February 2023

....

26
Now

*I am building for eternity
Stone by stone upon stone.
Everything a matter of time,
With time swiftly ticking away.
I will try to lay foundations for
Those who will tread after me.
I know I must because I must.
I do not control my tomorrow.
And tomorrow may never come
For me, but it will come for them.
And I can help them with theirs.
Bless the children who play,
Who run, who weep, who laugh,
Bless children who hunger for Love,
And those who thirst for life.
I will help them on this train of
Life that they are just getting on
And I will soon be getting off.
Someday may not exist in my
Tomorrow, for who knows what
God has ordained for my eternity.
There is only the here and now,
At least for me, as the seconds
Even now slowly tick away.
Because there is no "was" or
"Then," but only "now" for me.*

(REE, 6 August 2022)

....

27

A TESTIMONIAL about my father, and also about other Filipino prisoners of war of WW II on the occasion of Linggo Ng Kagitingan:

SOMEONE OF INTERNATIONAL POLITICAL PROMINENCE, A FORMER PRESIDENT OF THE UNITED STATES ONCE SAID ANYONE WHO WAS A PRISONER OF WAR IS A SUCKER, A LOSER.

WHAT IDIOCY!

At the outbreak of WW II, my father, Dr Rafael L Evangelista, volunteered to join the USAFFE medical corps. My father and others like him were captured in Bataan & Corregidor. But they were NOT LOSERS AND SUCKERS! How could they be when they fought and gave their lives for the most noble of causes, Freedom?

Why were these soldiers captured? NOT BECAUSE THEY WERE LOSERS OR SUCKERS! They were captured because promised reinforcements never came. Because many were armed with WW I single shot weapons which jammed in the mud and rain. Because many had pith, rather than steel, helmets. Because they had no tanks, armor, and modern planes. Because they did not have adequate training, ammunition, food or medicine.

But they held on in Bataan longer than they were expected to, derailing the schedule of Japan to conquer South East Asia, and, some say, from helping Germany in the fight against Russia. The Filipino soldiers changed the complexion of WW II, so that Bataan was not a defeat, but was the first critical step to ultimate victory. The Filipino Soldier in Bataan & Corrgidor, despite the surrender, was NOT A LOSER OR A SUCKER!

My father, as a doctor, risked his life to search for edible food and medicinal herbs for the troops in the Bataan countrysides, at times by sneaking behind enemy lines. After Bataan fell, he was imprisoned in Capas and Bilibid for months. Upon his release by the Japanese, he travelled north to work with and treat Filipino guerrillas and American stragglers in the mountains of the Cordilleras, Benguet, Nueva Ecija, Nueva Vizcaya, and Isabela.

He was arrested and tortured in Baguio by the Kempetai to force him to reveal the locations of the guerrilla bands. My earliest recollection at 4 years old of my father was of him strapped to the ceiling of the jail by his thumbs, bloodied, unconscious, and badly injured. Despite the torture, they never broke my father. MY FATHER WAS NOT A LOSER OR SUCKER!

My father was awarded the US Prisoner of War Medal. Later, he was awarded XXXosthumously the US Congressional Gold Medal. In my heart, I feel my father deserved much, much more, considering the wounds and scars he bore. What recognition he received was scant and belated, but it was recognition of his heroism nevertheless. MY FATHER WAS NOT A LOSER OR A SUCKER!

He and his Filipino companions did more for the cause of Freedom in Bataan & Corregidor than the critics who never fought in any war. My father did not evade war by claiming to have bone spurs or some disability. He volunteered to serve without ever having been conscripted! HE WAS NOT A LOSER OR A SUCKER!

As a member of a Congressional Gold Medal family and a proud descendant of a GENUINE WW II HERO, I stand proudly by the record of my father: MY FATHER, AND HIS COMPATRIOTS, WERE NOT SUCKERS OR LOSERS!

Remember our War Heroes of WW II!

RAFAEL E EVANGELISTA Immediate Past National Commander of the Defenders Of Bataan & Corregidor, (12 April 2023)

....

28
A Prayer of Love and Acknowledgement

Dear Jesus:
You are my Lord, my Master, my King.
In everything I think, do and say, let
Your Will be done.
You are my Savior, and my God.
I kneel before You and pay
You homage, because by
Your Holy Cross you have
redeemed me and the world.
I fear not,
I am not dismayed, for
You are my God.
You uphold me with
Your righteous Hand.
You are the Lamb of God
who takes away the sins of mankind.
Agnus Dei, qui tollis peccata mundi,
miserere nobis.
Have mercy on me.
Forgive me my sins.
Heal me.
Love me.
You are my Good Shepherd.
You lead me to green pastures,
and guide me to the
gates of Paradise.
When I am lost,
You search for me
and shelter me
in Your bosom.
You warm me in

Your embrace.
Your are my Pastor and
High Priest.
Your Consecrated Body and
Blood that You shed on the
Cross nourishes me with
the promise of eternal life.
Lord, I am not worthy that
You should come into my heart.
Say the word, and I shall be healed.
You, My Lord, have configured me in
Your Image when
You gave Your Life for me upon the Tree.
You are the Resurrection and the Life.
You are my Lamp, my Light,
my Life, my Love, my All.
I offer my heart and soul to You.
See me safely through this moment,
through this day, through this life.
I love You, Lord Jesus.
I love You!
Amen!

(Raf Evangelista, 17 March 2023, Based on Scriptural Readings)

....

29
Haiku Questions On Love

Where is heaven now?
Has God removed it from reach?
Or is it my fault?

Why is there hell on
Earth with heaven out of reach?

Will all men be damned?

Is today for naught?
How I long for yesterday
When love came to be.

I will keep trying
To reach my God, even as
He Reaches out to me.

Be still, my heart.
Know That He is your Almighty,
Who is perfect love.

It has been so long
That I have knelt in prayer
To honor my Lord.

Our Father in heaven,
I am sorry for my sins.
Let Thy kingdom come.

But there is love too
In the beauty of today.
Look to God's heavens!

In the wood's darkness,
Listen to the winds whisper:
Believe! God is here!

And blue skies echo
The soft songs of the heavens:
God is here! He is!

Inside my soul's depths,
I hear His voice gently say:
Look here in your heart!

If I hold Your Hand,

Will you guide where Love is …
Love that never fades.

(Raf Evangelista, 12 March 2023)

....

30
Cory and Noynoy - Democracy By Public Servanthood

On the eve of the anniversary of the People's Power Revolution on February 25, 1986, we may wish to contemplate on the following:

There were significant differences between the presidencies of the two Aquinos and some other presidencies. The circumstances were quite different and extraordinary. And impressively, the two presidencies of Cory and Pnoy were not dynasties at all.

1. There was NO AMBITION. Ninoy was the politician; Cory and children led quiet lives. Simple lives. They lived in Times Street QC, starkly different from the Forbes Park residences of their cousins. Cory was no socialite. Her routine was never that of the blue ladies of lore. She picked up her children in school and was a hands-on mom. The children were low-profile achievers, magagaling pero mapagkumbaba, walang wang-wang.

2. Events unfolded, something that can not be orchestrated by mere mortals or even by the most astute politician. The Powerful miscalculated, the evil of the avaricious ironically unleashed a more powerful force - an awakened people. It was as if a Divine Hand led Cory and PNoy to a place not of their own choosing. But they were the chosen and the anointed to lead.

2. Cory and PNoy did NOT COVET POWER, they were thrust into it. They did not want it; but they and

family had to go in deep prayer to discern God's Will, and they came out of it with a willingness to serve.

3. When Cory was in midterm of her presidency, Noynoy approached her about his intention of running as Tarlac congressman. "Not in my term" said Cory. Noynoy did not run. Clearly it was not AMBITION nor POWER-TRIPPING that fueled his desire to serve.

4. After their respective terms, there was an uneventful changing of guard, and they returned to their unassuming abode in Times St. as ordinary citizens.

5. Cory assumed the presidency under a revolutionary government (People Power). She had an option to run a new term but she chose not to. PNoy did not initiate Charter Change or amendments that would have extended his term (unlike FVR, GMA and Du30). They served to the best of their abilities - Cory to restore the democracy that had been hijacked, and PNoy to rebuild the democratic institutions that had been corrupted.

6. They did not enrich themselves while in power. They knew they had a legacy to protect. Beyond that, they literally considered themselves Servants of the People.

If people can not make out what all that was - I'll spell it out ... DEMOCRACY by PUBLIC SERVANTHOOD.

But it is our failing if we did not take cognizance of the suffering, the sacrifice, the hard work the Aquinos went through for our country. Some have demonized them, ridiculed decency, laughed at matuwid na daan. And that's why we are in a shithole now.

And that is our Nation's loss! Raf Evangelista,

(A former next door neighbor of the Aquinos On Times St, QC) 23 February 2023

....

31
THE SACRIFICE OF LOVE (A Poem Honoring Filipino veterans who served in WW II in the Philippines)

We salute our vets,
We salute our flags,
As we now remember ...
For love, some sacrificed some...
And others sacrificed all!

Prayers from our hearts,
Blossoms on the ground,
White crosses that remind ...
Many sacrificed some...
And many sacrificed all!

Our country 'tis to thee,
Our land of liberty,
That to our fathers gave ...
Some sacrificing some...
Some sacrificing all!

We now stand proud and tall
By warmth of freedom blessed,
Because they marched before...
In pitched battle risking some...
In throes of death giving all!

If today, the air around is free
And the skies above are clear,
Remember there were those...
Who for love gave some...
While others gave their all!

Straighten wayward crosses,
Plant flowers on their graves,

Say a prayer for them who were
Wounded, died... or forgotten...
Who gave some... or maybe all!

Do not let their pictures fade,
In our hearts, or minds, or homes.
Tell the children of the heroes...
Who risked their lives for them...
Sacrificing blood... or life for all!

(Rafael E. Evangelista, December 29, 2019)

....

32
Configurations of a Democracy - Vision of Manny Valdehuesa

Manny Valdehuesa truly believed in the GBM slogan that called for the empowerment of the people at the grassroots. The slogan reads: "Without the direct democracy of the Small Barangay Republic, the legitimacy of our government and political system will always be suspect."

Manny insisted that GBM must be committed to democratic methods even as it works for revolutionary change. Manny constantly urged Filipinos to reform their sovereign role in the governance of their small Barangay republics, all 42,000 plus of them. He urged them to take control of their Barangays, a revolutionary change of political mind set even now.

Reconfigured around these 42,000 + Barangays, Manny's vision was that the Republic's superstructure would assume a pyramidal shape with 3 layers:

1. The primary layer and broad base of our Democracy - these 42,000 + Barangay governments;

2. The intermediate layer - the 1,600 + municipal and provincial governments; and

3. The top layer - the national government located at the pyramid's peak.

The primary layer, or broad base of the political pyramid, Manny always said, is supposed to stabilize the overall government vertical symmetry and balance, if Democracy is to survive.

On the other hand, a government where all power emanates from the national layer is bound to be unstable, standing as it would on the apex of the pyramid. And oftentimes this inverted pyramid translates to dictatorship and autocratic rule.

People empowerment was a vision that Manny shared with President Ramon Magsaysay, who he admired. Magsaysay wrote, "I believe that the government starts at the bottom and moves upward, for government exists basically for the welfare of the masses of the Nation."

Manny's vision is echoed in the 1987 Constitution which states that "Sovereignty resides in the people and all governmental authority emanates from them."

His vision is reflected in the Local Government Code which provides for a parliamentary form of government at the Barangay level, with the Barangay Assembly as the de facto parliament, the highest official political, cultural and social body in the Barangay. And who comprise the Barangay Assembly? All the Barangay residents, the People.

Manny talked about People Empowerment as early as the mid 1960s. He was a visionary long before People Empowerment was embodied in the Constitution. He used to visit me in Washington DC where I partnered in the International Law Firm of Baker & McKenzie. Manny's favorite conversation points centered on his "People Empowerment" experiences in Israel's kibutzes and Switzerland's cantons.

However, it was really in mid 1998 that Gising Barangay was born. As Manny himself wrote in an article published by Google, "It was then that a former UN executive from Mindanao and a lawyer banker from Manila actively started toying with the idea of a grass roots movement to promote an assertive brand of citizen sovereignty." That UN executive was, of course, Manny, and the lawyer banker just happened to be me.

But then, it bothered Manny that some consider the 1986 People Power Revolution, and hence by extrapolation the 1987 Constitution, as failures in people empowerment.

Is that so?

Manny and I also had discussions on this issue.

Manny and I believed that EDSA was an unfinished, not a failed, revolution. We believed that there had to be five stages to complete it:

1. The Revolt itself;

2. A new Constitution and implementing laws;

3. Education and involvement of the people in the empowerment process, specially at Barangay level;

4. Election of competent, trustworthy and knowlegeable officials, at Barangay level, who believe in people empowerment; and

5. Establishment of model barangays in various regions of the Philippines.

Of these five stages, only the first two have been accomplished.

Why?

A survey some years ago revealed that the People empowerment provisions of the Constitution and implementing laws are ignored or poorly understood by government officials. And to make things worse, their constituents know little or nothing about them, specially their role in the Barangay's governing process. These are the main reasons why the EDSA Revolution is still unfinished. To this day, few understand what a "Public Servant" truly means.

Reflecting on the GBM slogan that we are committed to, GBM still has its work cut out for it, now more than ever. There is obviously still much to be done to complete our role in the People Power Revolution.

I am sure that Manny, by God's will, is cheering GBM on towards the completion of the Revolution, and the vision of grassroot governance that he was such a staunch advocate of.

In closing, let me say that it has been an honor and privilege to have been associated with Manny for the past 56 years. Manny,

I salute you!

Raf Evangelista 17 September 2021

....

33
Trust

Don't allow heartaches to get control unto you. Seek God's guidance pray for serenity. Focus on goals . Worrying can do no good to our health . We must understand that there are things we cannot control. It is then that we must have the serenity to accept the things we cannot change, the courage to strive for the things we can, and the wisdom to know the difference.

The sad past is essentially depression. Eliminate it and adjust yourself. Life without struggle is like a car without wheels. Remove self tormenting of the past. Empower yourself not dwell on unchangeable. No more fighting unwinnable wars . Stay firm when criticized for doing the unpopular, but right, thing. The is one way to increase your value .You cannot stop world's criticism but you can learn to be tough emotionally. You can't change the direction of the wind but you can always adjust your sail. Make your life better. Time in this planet is limited . It's not easy but it will be worth it to trust your intuition. Challenge yourself. Explore, train & discover. Enforce discipline and trust the process.

....

34
I AM WHO AM THIS CHRISTMAS AND THE NEW YEAR

I AM this very moment.
I AM today,
I am this Year.
I AM your past,
I am your future.
I AM the fresh page in your book of time.
I AM the Wisdom to make sense of
all failures and sorrows.
I AM the
Fount of all joy and happiness.
All the blessings that you sought and
did not find is in the
Palm of My Hand,
All the good that you tried
but did not achieve,
All that you dreamed
but did not dare to do,
All that you hoped but did not will,
All the faith that you claimed
but did not have,
I AM the Power to make them
all come true.
I AM the Word.
I AM the Eucharist.
I AM Love.
I AM the One
who makes all things new.
I AM Jesus,

your Christmas and
your New Life.
I Am Your New Year!
Come, and be blessed by Me!

(Raf Evangelista, 23 December 2022)

....

35
An Ode to a Loved One:

Sharing a poem that I wrote many years ago. I hope this poem will remind you of the beautiful times you had with ones you loved … and who are now gone.

- An Ode to a Loved One:

Fly Angel, Fly
Even in the gathering
Shadows of dusk,
When death had lost
All its terror,
You welcomed
The new dawn to come

With much relief.
And when I asked you softly,
Surely with tears
Welling in my eyes,
If you had to go,
You nodded gently.

With a flicker
Of the sunset
On your beautiful face
One more time,

*You smiled in
One last goodbye.*

*Then you were gone,
Like the colored scent
Of a bouquet of
Evening blossoms
Spiraling heavenwards
To the waiting sunrise.*

And so, in a last adieu, I say…

*Why do I continue to love you,
Even if I do not try?
Why do I continue to remember
When I can no longer cry?
But then you never doubted
Even as you said goodbye.
So fly on, my Angel, fly.*

*You looked after
The garden of my soul.
You nurtured it,
You kept it whole.
Who will watch over it
Now that you are gone?
Will the fates care for it
Just as you have done?*

*You made each friend feel special,
Each friend who felt your touch.
They tell me how you cared for them,
Each one, so very much.
I can believe your friends,
All those who tell me this.
I too have felt your warming touch
Like a lingering summer kiss.*

I found myself denying

Some thoughts I had of you,
In order to prevent the darkness
That threatened to break through.
I thought of all the happier times
That you and I have had,
And tried to forget the moment
When everything went sad.

Loving can never be easy
When one is grieving so,
But simply by denying,
Can one ever then let go?

As you sleep in the fading light,
I rejoice in the time we had together.
I gaze on visions of you fondly in
The night's stillness, and remember
How everything then was so right
In all the moments we had together,
Moments of life, of time, and of love
Cherished and nourished forever.
Sleep well, sleep tight, my Love,
To the embrace of God surrender.

Your summer kiss lingers
In the deepening autumn of life,
Whether in good times or in bad,
In happiness or in strife,
Calling two hearts together,
Even as it did back then,
With scents of spring's coming,
Not simply where but when.

I do continue to love you,
I do not have to try.
I will continue to remember,
Though I no longer cry.
You never doubted God's love,
Even when you said,

"Goodbye."
So fly on, my Angel, fly!

(Rafael E. Evangelista, 4 November 2004)

....

36
Living With Joy, And Being A Man For Others

One can count his age and consider the total days and years as his compendium of life. But life means much more. Life is a myriad of teachings and learnings. It is a tale of life-changing lessons with a touch of laughter and happiness, and a touch of tears and sadness. The jokes and sad tales shared with others are mirrors of reality. But the humor and joy that come with life makes us realize that one can maintain positivity in any situation. Ultimately, life successfully spent is about dwelling on the smiles and laughter, while learning from the frowns and tears. Life is about focusing on kindness and selflessness, rather than personal gain and greed.

Through it all, the best thing that we must learn is that focusing and dwelling on the sad and ugly things as a disgruntled bystander in the corner is no way to live life. One must dream dreams, aim high, take risks, be bold, all for the sake of joyous righteousness. Risk-taking for good is not an impulsive act but rather an act of deliberately trying and learning, and thus becoming a better version of oneself. And in this process, one will understand that life is best Spirit led. This is what ultimately brings true joy, peace and good humor. This is what life should be all about - reveling in the joy of being a Man For God And Others. (Raffy Evangelista, 11 September 2022)

....

37
THANK YOU, LORD

Thank you, Lord, for every "little thing":
-the rays of hope a smile can bring,
-the clasp of a loving, helping hand,
-the soothing comfort of "I understand,"
-the warmth of the sun after the rain,
-the calming comfort after the pain,
-friends that stay midst trials and tears,
-the peace GOD gives to calm our fears,
-for all His mercy and His love,
-and prayers answered from above!
Oct 13, 2022

....

38
The Value Of The Gift

It is the value of things that counts, not the price. There is a big difference between value and price. As we hurry along to catch special day deadlines and buy gifts for the many on our gift lists, let us reflect on how many of the gifts we intend to give out are motivated by love or friendship. The kiss of a loved one has more value than a pricey gift given without love.

And the most valuable love gift we will ever receive is Jesus. It is for this reason that we can't, we shouldn't, take Christ out of our gift giving, because

Jesus is the ultimate gift. He came to sacrifice His life for us to save us. His was the supreme sacrifice of love, His invaluable gift of life to us in exchange for His own on the Cross.

May our Lord Jesus be with you everyday of the rest of your life. God bless you always. (Raffy Evangelista, 11 December 2022)

....

39
My Prayer Today

Today I begin to see the sun set,
Even as I was born to its rising.
I ask not for a remaining life
That is trouble or trial free.
Lord,
You asked me in my younger years
To pick up my cross and follow You.
I did not always do so, and never answered
You with an open heart.
And so now with all contriteness, all
I ask for is the grace of fortitude,
hope and perseverance to do only
What You will, even as I move with
Awe, wonder and anticipation
Towards the colors of the sun.
In all things, may only
Your Will be Done, and in the glorious sunset,
May I find the Light of the Lord!
Lux in Domino!
Amen!

Rafael E Evangelista 8 October 2022

....

40
When

I have spread my roots,
And I no longer fear the rain,
Even if my heart still beats
Against the surging grain.

Beneath dark clouds
And winds unseen,
My heart still asks what
Might or could have been.

Times ago, darkness came
From shadows of distant hills.
In those moments my heart
Froze to fears and chills.

Undertows threatened
The oceans where I'd been.
I could not ignore forces
That swept in unseen.

But I know there is a sun.
I truly believe it will return
To my Country and shine
On life's every twist and turn.

Roots will stand firm again
As they have stood before.
My tree will grow in faith …
My country to restore!

Sunshine will rule my sky

And dark will then be gone.
God is simply guiding me.
My story is not yet done.

Have faith, the Lord tells me.
Sunshine will come one day.
"When"is for God to decide …
Then love will come to stay.

Raffy Evangelista 17 June 2022

....

41
The Wedding of Miguel and Mela Jayme

Remembering and sharing some beautiful memories from some years ago of a very special wedding
- the wedding of Miguel and Mela Jayme,

Where I spoke thus:
"I would like to start off by reading a poem, then my exhortation, and finally a prayer. Please bear with me as I exercise the prerogative of speaking a little longer than he should about a couple he loves dearly:

THE POEM –
Fr James F Donelan SJ, an authority on English Literature, calls this poem the most famous love poem in the English language. Despite the poem's apparent simplicity, it is as profound in what is said, as in what remained unsaid. Elizabeth Barrett Browning lived a life-long love for her husband, a love that gave all and asked for nothing. I will read the poem for our newly weds:

How Do I Love Thee

How do I love thee?
Let me count the ways:
I love thee to the depth and
breadth and height
My soul can reach.
I love thee to the level of
everyday's most quiet need,
By sun and candlelight.
I love thee with the breath,
Smiles, tears of all my life!
And if God choose,
I shall but love thee
better after death.

A STEPFATHER'S MESSAGE

Mela and Migs, please understand that God asked you in Church today to pledge to each other an unconditional love much like Elizabeth Browning's.

Mela, I realize that even as I watched you grow, one day I would have to let you go. Today as you hitch your wagon to an exciting new world with Migs, I shall step aside so you can do so unconditionally.

From today, you must invest your heart and soul in your new endeavor - to be a loving life partner to Migs, a caring mother to your future children, and a good and devoted daughter to Cecile and Juny. Love them all without condition or reservation.

Never say "never" to your marriage, so that, with the support and love of Migs, your marriage will remain "forever." Marriage is a portrait that you and Migs can make beautiful, from literally millions of moments that will create your love story together. But you must work hard to make it so.

Pope Francis said of marriage: do not "dream of an idyllic and perfect love... Be realistic about your limits, defects, and imperfections, respond to the call to grow together, bring love to maturity, and strengthen the union, come what may."

Migs and Mela, love is a decision, not merely an instinct; marriage is hard work, not simply a pipe dream. Do not break a heart, and expect it to love. Do not break a soul, and tell it to be happy. Do not focus only on the worst, and ask the other to see only the good.

Unity in love may involve the struggle to stay united through difficult decisions: whether to stand firm or to stand down, together or individually. A mature marriage allows for a love that may require the sharing of one's mind, rather than simply the heart, even when the emotions dictate otherwise.

Building, giving, forgiving are keys to an abiding love. Do not expect your spouse's love to be a building love, if your own love is not one that gives. Do not expect your partner's love to be a giving love, if your own love is not forgiving. Build together, give to each other, forgive one another always, just as God always builds, gives and forgives in love.

Make prayer and God's Word the glue that binds your union together. The richness of love can be found not just in the glow of sunset and the embrace of one another, but also in the pacific solitude of prayer together. In everything in your marriage, throughout your marriage, seek God, ask God, thank God.

Migs, I entrust to your care a most beautiful person I have come to know and love. Please honor and love Mela with all your being, just as I expect her to honor and love you.

Migs, take Mela into your heart, into the Jayme family, into your circle of friends and influence. Mela, as you join the Jayme family, never forget your Rodrigo and Garcia roots, and the rich heritage they have bequeathed to you.

May God's calm and peace always be an integral part of this most permanent, lasting, and loving journey of your lives.

A PRAYER FOR THE NEWLY WEDS –

Finally, by way of a collective blessing for our newly weds, I would like you all to repeat after me this prayer inspired by Fr James B Reuter SJ:

Lord God, look down upon Mela and Migs.
/Give them the grace to consecrate their union entirely to You,
/all the actions of their bodies and souls.
/May all the thoughts that come to them be true, /may all the things to which their hearts go out /be beautiful with the beauty of God,
/may all the things they want be good. /In the unity of love and marriage,
/grant them the light to know Your will,
/the grace to embrace it, /the courage and strength to do it,
/we ask You this, through Christ, our Lord. Amen.

A FATHER'S BLESSING –

This has been an awesome day in your lives, Migs and Mela. From this day on, go and make an awesome life together! I love and bless you both!"
Pap (Raffy Evangelista, 23 February 2020)

....

42

Accountability And Empathy

Growing up, I learned that accountability doesn't come with age. In this life, you'll meet a lot of people who seem to be at the right age but aren't aware of accountability. People who only care about a problem when it already affects them. People who, among all, are expected to be mature enough to admit their mistakes and do something about it but do otherwise. In life you'll meet adults who will hold you accountable for their own lapses. And sometimes you have to bear with that.

Because accountability doesn't come with age, it should come with empathy. The ability to put yourself into someone else's shoes and look at life from where they're standing. Accountability should come from empathy because empathy makes you see how your carelessness will affect others. So instead of just sitting comfortably, unbothered by the chaos you know you played a part in, you stop making excuses for yourself and face your truth. You stop trying to negotiate that your intention was good and the outcome wasn't what you wanted. When you have empathy, you learn to take accountability over the consequences of your actions regardless of your intention. (Raffy Evangelista, 25 August 2022)

....

43
After The Pandemic And Beyond Politics - ONE!

Let us join hearts and minds and souls together as we travel through this current maelstrom of life. We must believe that we are one in God, that we are one in spirit, one under one flag, that We are One, if we are to survive.

Our objective through all the confusion and hurt of this pandemic and concurrent debilitating politics is to produce a citizenry that appreciates and is conscious of it nationhood and has national goals for the betterment of the community, and not an anarchic mass of people who know how to take care of themselves only.

We must build a new nation that can survive its fools, and even the ambitious. But more, we must not tolerate treason from within - persons who speak in accents familiar to their victims, who appeal to the baseness that lies deep in the hearts of men. For they rot the soul of the nation. They infect the body politic so that it can no longer resist. Murderers are less to be feared.

And when this twin evil of this pandemic and rotten politics is done, we must vow as one never to again approach a bull from the front, a horse from the rear, or an idiot from any direction. We have had many idiots leading us through this pandemic. And we shall replace the sign where we so meekly pleaded for years, "Please Do not disturb", with one that warns our would be leaders, "Already disturbed. Proceed with caution!"

Look out at our horizons. This pandemic has brought cleaner air, less traffic and pollution. That is at least one positive effect that this pandemic has brought to our environment. There is no reason why our country and people cannot come together and grab the opportunities that this pandemic brings to also cleanse our political way of life.

We will prayerfully come after this pandemic together as one with the understanding that nationalism that arises from populist myopia cannot always be equated with patriotism, heroism or love of country. We are, we must be, One! (REE, 29 April 2020)

....

44

I Am Your Brother, We Are Kin

Sometimes the peace
Of evening nightfall
Sits lovelier than the
Brillance of the
Morning sunrise.
Join hands with me
Once more and stay
By my side again.
Even as shadows
Now appear in the
Fading sunset, and
Despite threatening
Clouds and passing
Fierce rainstorms,
You are my brother
And I am yours.
You are my brother
In Christ, and
I always will be.

(REE, 10 August 2022)

....

45
Make A Stand Now (On The Occasion of National Heroes' Day)

Death of the sinagtala,
Death of the fireflies in the skies
Death of the rainbows
Death of the wind's gentle sighs.

*What happened to our world before
When wrong and evil came to power,
Can happen again if we fail to fight!
Our children, their families will suffer!*

*Some feign ignorance and disaffection.
How can they sit back and not even dare?
Our heroes died in the field of sacrifice.
Beyond fearful, we just do not care!*

*On our land, the sun will either rise or set.
What is it that we wish to preside over?
If we do not now have the backbone,
The sunrise could be lost forever.*

*The sun disappeared from sight before.
Shall we let darkness set on us again?
But that is what our country is facing
Unless we make a stand now, not when.*

*Dream of rainbows shining in the night,
Of the sun forever lighting up our day.
Let us stand strong together as one
And let God's bidding guide our way.*

*"Para sa Diyos at Bayan," our cry,
In glorious battle and blessed peace.
Bring back the sinagtala, and rainbows …
A love of Bayan that will never cease.*

(Raffy Evangelista, 28 November 2021)

46

Truth, and not Vox Populi, is the Voice of God.

Contrary to popular belief, "Vox Populi, Vox Dei" is not a Church doctrine.

Yes, we are told to respect authority and public officials. Yes, we are told to follow the law and to work for the common good of our respective communities and nations. And yes, we are also taught to value democracy and all its fruits: the recognition of human rights and dignity, and the power of the ballot, among others.

But there are times when Vox Populi, the Voice of the People - even if they speak in astounding unison - cannot and should not be mistaken for the Voice of God. There are times when people are misled by lies, or threatened by force, or rewarded for believing what they know to be untrue.

I think this is very relevant as we reconcile ourselves with the outcome of the past national elections. Not merely because we are disappointed with its results, but rather because we are concerned with what they mean for us as a country moving forward.

What many of us find most concerning is our relationship with truth. The advent of social media has made the spreading of information easier and more convenient, but it has not made the information more reliable. Throughout these elections, many problematic opinions and downright false news and information have proliferated in order to attack certain people and lift up others.

Of course, this is nothing new. Studies from reputable academic institutions have noted the prominent role of YouTube, Facebook, TikTok, and Twitter in increasing the media reach of national politicians in providing "alternative facts" related to the political history of this country.

Many of us are also no strangers to the fact that many relationships have been fractured by debates and discussions on what is true and what should be believed, and the actions which historical facts should entail. We feel the frustration in many persons who, upon wholeheartedly trying to convince the other to not fall for lies on the internet, have met with a dismissive plea to "respect" the other person's "opinion."

So we try to understand why people find some truths hard to accept. Sometimes, it isn't just because of doubt. Sometimes, it's because of fear. Accepting one truth, if we are being honest with ourselves, will force us to accept other truths, which may even be more difficult to accept. For example, some find it difficult to accept that some politician stole millions from the country because they lived quite bountifully during that politician's term.

For those people, accepting that people were dying of hunger and violence while they lived in privilege would mean that they should accept that they benefited from such dark times. And that all the time they spent actively denying and defending those historical facts would have been cruel, unjust, and downright evil.

Accepting truth can also be uncomfortable because it demands specific actions and changes from us. One cannot live an honest life without acting on the truths that he or she learns. For example, if one seeks to be an honest person who believes that all people deserve dignity and respect, then he must always respect and listen to everyone: even those with whom he disagrees. Believing something to be true and acting on it can be difficult and inconvenient.

That's why many of us just settle for half-truths. Half-truths do not require a lot from us. Only that we keep telling ourselves and other people those half-truths. For example, we can believe the truth that the minimum wage should be raised for people to cope with increasing prices, but also believe the lie that we don't have to picket and petition the government to increase it. That way, we don't have to join unions or organize rallies or attend meetings. Believing some truths while buying into some lies keeps us from committing to meaningful action.

There are many of us now who are struggling to forgive those who have bought into blatant lies and half-truths of the last elections. We find it hard to believe that a son of a deposed leader, who actively denies the injustices and crimes his family has committed, has won based on and in spite of his family's legacy. We find it hard to accept that we live in a society that approves of violence against our fellow citizens. That tolerates human rights abuses in the name of discipline. That perpetuates lies about the human and economic cost of political regimes.

But perhaps it is our turn to accept such hard truths. And to accept what they mean. Maybe it is our turn to accept that life was not so different for many of us under former political regimes. That poverty and abuse of power remained rampant and acceptable regardless of who the President was. That desperation has turned the elections into an opportunity to earn extra money, even if it means giving power to the undeserving. That, maybe, we ourselves have not been good examples of authority and power to our children and relatives.

They say "vox populi, vox Dei." But that is often not the case. After all, the same people who welcomed Jesus when he entered Jerusalem were likely the same people who called for his crucifixion. Our faith believes that God speaks in numbers of ways: through His Commandments, through the actions of His Son, the deeds of His followers, and sometimes, even through "a still, small, voice." But here's the thing: He never speaks in lies.

Whether or not the last elections have brought to power the people we wanted, it is incumbent upon us, as Christians, as Church people, as members of the labor movement, and as citizens to use this time to reflect and listen. What is the God of Truth trying to say to us? What are we required to do to correct the injustices of the past? And upon hearing what that Voice has to say, it is our task to speak the Truth, no matter how different it may be from the lies which some claim is the Voice of the People, Vox Populi. (REE, 10 August 2022)

....

47
Pillars Of The Family

The path to the healing and unity of a family is truth, love, empathy, fairness and justice. Without any of these pillars, the family will disintegrate, leaving each member alone to follow his or her path. Pity the generations who follow after. (REE, 10 August 2022)

....

48
I Love You

Have you noticed
The darkest night
Can lead to the
brightest light?

And the stillness
Of listless skies
To ballads of winds
In melodic sighs?

I often dream of you
From stunning sunset
To shimmering dawn as
Now I dream of you yet.

*I never realized
My darkest night
Would lead to you …
To morn and sunlight.*

*You have returned
The beauty of song
To my restless ways.
Now I truly belong.*

*Beyond shadowy hills
And gathering haze,
You have brought light
To my remaining days.*

*May gold color your dusk,
And may it color your day,
May ballads continue to sing,
For you forever I pray!*

I love you!

(Raf Evangelista, 30 July 2022)

....

49
Time Passing

*There was a time,
In the heavy fog,
The shadowy trees started
To sway in the dark
As the wind picked up
That old mournful song:
"Where have all*

The flowers gone,
Long time passing…
Gone to graveyards
Every one…
And I asked myself,
When will I ever learn?
When will I ever learn?
The flowers were gone;
The birds were gone;
The sunshine was gone.
It is dark all over.

But then, In the dark,
I saw
Your face, saw the light,
And saw
Forever.
The sun is back,
The flowers bloom,
The zephyrs sing
A joyous song.
What has changed?
Forever has changed.
It is not darkness.
For Light has come.
It is no longer just Now,
For love has changed.
I fell in love with you,
Not just with my eyes
But with my heart.
And despite the dark,
And passage of time,
I know my heart will
Never change,
For it had found
True love, and it is
Light forever.

And it is not

Just how I feel.
But how you feel
Is what is so
Important to me.
The look in your
Eyes says that
You love me,
And that is eternity
To me.
It is the Now
That makes the blooms
Sing a different refrain:
Where have all
The flowers gone?
Gone to lovers
Everyone, and
I Will never change.
Why should I ever
Change, long Time passing?

(REE, 25 July 2022)

....

50
Barangay Governance

Let's take advantage of the available, albeit narrowing democratic space on the matter of governance. We have the opportunity and the right to participate in our barangay governance and improve such governance at the grassroots, especially among the grossly disadvantaged, in our midst.

Register as voters in Marikina if not yet registered, and then register as members of your barangay assemblies in your respective barangays. Then help organize and educate your barangays.

Please note that despite the 2x/yr limitation on the number of barangay assemblies declared by Malacanang sometime ago, barangay assemblies may be held more often at the discretion of the barangay residents or as may be provided by the Local Government Code.

Registering as voters will allow us to vote for all responsible and knowledgeable barangay servant leaders. Let us also all become members of our respective assemblies so that we can have direct participation in the governance of our barangays. Let us participate in the activities of our local development councils which are primarily tasked to prepare the regular development plans of our barangay. These barangay development plans ultimately are supposed to form part of the National development plan. (Raf Evangelista, 2022)

....

51

Opening Remarks - The Barangay and How It Relates to Mater et Magistra (the encyclical on Church/Christianity and Social Progress - St Pope John Paul XXIII)

Over the years, we have been faced with "the erosion of the anthropological foundations which ground the possibility of civil society." What we are facing is "a situation where the indispensable bases for an authentically democratic and Christian society have been radically undermined.

What are the anthropological foundations of civil society? Basically they are four: truth, justice, peace, love. These foundations have been violently shaken. Thus, 1) In the conduct of public affairs truth has been badly battered. People have learned to believe as true the exact opposite of what is officially announced. And when the untruth is made public it is hypocritically given the semblance of an honorable disguise. 2) Justice has been brutalized beyond recognition. The lady of justice has been stripped of her blindfold and the balance scales are often replaced by the truncheon or by the barrel of a gun. 3)The meaning of peace has been distorted. Peace has come to mean the desolation of a hamletted village or the grim visage of a silenced salvage victim. 4) Love at best has come to manifest itself in the shape of wasteful display and at worst in human sacrifice at the altar of national security.

And it is in this critical context that we, the people, are challenged to make a contribution. We have been, by God's grace, provided with a vehicle to achieve and reinstall the four foundations of civil society in our country. That vehicle is the barangay. Today, let us ask ourselves. What is it that we as Filipinos can offer to our communities and our country to achieve the social progress espoused by Pope John Paul XX III?

One answer we can offer our people is "the barangay," and all it explicitly and implicitly implies!

But "what, why, how" the barangay is for us to learn about and to implement in each of our communities.

We have much still to learn and understand! (Raf Evangelista, 2022)

....

52

CONSTITUTION OF THE REPUBLIC OF THE PHILIPPINES AND STATUTORY PROVISIONS ON SERVANT LEADERSHIP

Aside from the Preamble of the Constitution that provides: "Sovereignty resides in the people, and all governmental authority emanates from them" and the Lincolnesque statement that "Democracy is a government of the people, for the people, and by the people," other relevant legal references on servant leadership are:

ARTICLE XI Accountability of Public Officers

SECTION 1. Public office is a public trust. Public officers and employees must at all times be accountable to the people, serve them with utmost responsibility, integrity, loyalty, and efficiency, act with patriotism and justice, and lead modest lives.

RA 6713 Code of Conduct and Ethical Standards for Public Officials and Employees

Section 4. Norms of Conduct of Public Officials and Employees. - (A) Every public official and employee shall observe the following as standards of personal conduct in the discharge and execution of official duties:

(a) Commitment to public interest. - Public officials and employees shall always uphold the public interest over and above personal interest. All government resources and powers of their respective offices must be employed and used efficiently, effectively, honestly and economically, particularly to avoid wastage in public funds and revenues.

(b) Professionalism. - Public officials and employees shall perform and discharge their duties with the highest degree of excellence, professionalism, intelligence and skill. They shall enter public service with utmost devotion and dedication to duty. They shall endeavor to discourage wrong perceptions of their roles as dispensers or peddlers of undue patronage.

(c) Justness and sincerity. - Public officials and employees shall remain true to the people at all times. They must act with justness and sincerity and shall not discriminate against anyone, especially the poor and the underprivileged. They shall at all times respect the rights of others, and shall refrain from doing acts contrary to law, good morals, good customs, public policy, public order, public safety and public interest. They shall not dispense or extend undue favors on account of their office to their relatives whether by consanguinity or affinity except with respect to appointments of such relatives to positions considered strictly confidential or as members of their personal staff whose terms are coterminous with theirs.

(d) Political neutrality. - Public officials and employees shall provide service to everyone without unfair discrimination and regardless of party affiliation or preference.

(e) Responsiveness to the public. - Public officials and employees shall extend prompt, courteous, and adequate service to the public. Unless otherwise provided by law or when required by the public interest, public officials and employees shall provide information of their policies and procedures in clear and understandable language, ensure openness of information, public consultations and hearings whenever appropriate, encourage suggestions, simplify and systematize policy, rules and procedures, avoid red tape and develop an understanding and appreciation of the socio-economic conditions prevailing in the country, especially in the depressed rural and urban areas.

(f) Nationalism and patriotism. - Public officials and employees shall at all times be loyal to the Republic and to the Filipino people, promote the use of locally produced goods, resources and technology and encourage appreciation and pride of country and people.

They shall endeavor to maintain and defend Philippine sovereignty against foreign intrusion.

(g) Commitment to democracy. - Public officials and employees shall commit themselves to the democratic way of life and values, maintain the principle of public accountability, and manifest by deeds the supremacy of civilian authority over the military. They shall at all times uphold the Constitution and put loyalty to country above loyalty to persons or party.

(h) Simple living. - Public officials and employees and their families shall lead modest lives appropriate to their positions and income. They shall not indulge in extravagant or ostentatious display of wealth in any form. Public Office Is A Public Trust!

(Raf Evangelista, 1997)

....

53
Sunset of Darkness

The sun has come down
Again as it did once before
Without its beautiful sunset.
My anguished soul cries out:
"Tis to thee sweet land of
Liberty, to thee I sing:
land Of the morning, child of the
Sun returning, be thou morning
Blessed, be thou sun caressed!"
My tears shall water the land,
This land my forebearers
Have lived and died for ...

Perlas ng silanganan, Duyan ng magiting,
Sa manlulupig, di ka pasisiil.
Where has the sun gone?

*Will the land be sunrise
Blessed again?
I cry out in The darkness that has
Vanquished the sunset ..,
"For now, I shout out my Prayer …
only for now!"*

Raffy Evangelista 29 May 2022

....

54
Real Love, The Day He Died

*His Love turned darkness
Into brightness of pure Light.
His Splendor banished sadness
And the loneliness of night.*

*The perfect Love Day is not
What man declares it to be.
True Love occured before that
When He was nailed to the tree.*

*Blood flowed from His Heart above,
As He hang dying on that tree,
He bought our lives with
His love, Removing sin from you and me.*

*Perfect love He gave us when He died.
Revealing how much He truly cared.
Can we spread love, can we even try,
The way He gave, the way He shared?*

*Sharing love is all He asks we give.
"Give love as I give you life,"
He said; "Eternity I shared, you have received,*

Give to others before the sun is fled."

*The real Love Day is when He gave
His Love to free both you and me,
And sacrificed His Life to save all
That one distant day on Calvary.*

(REE, 15 April 2022) Happy Love Day,
this April 15, 2022 to all - Good Friday –
when Jesus proved that
He loves us all! God bles

....

55
WE ARE SPINNING
(In the maelstrom of corruption)

*Our country is spinning In tyrannical cycles.
This island home we're in
Turns in dangerous circles.*

*Day in, day out,
Where are we going?
Beyond the turnabouts,
Dark winds are blowing.*

*Turning and turning,
Blowing to a spinning spin.
We are stumbling, fleeing,
In and out, and out and in.*

*No longer any rhyme or
Reason to frenetic turns,
Unmindful of scraping, falling
And those painful burns.*

Dizzying, dizzying, dizzying.

How, where, and when to go?
Here to there, to anywhere,
Our tyrant rulers blunder so!

To some, the evil is not real.
If so, what then is false or true?
Who then is to ask: who lies?
Is it me, or the devil in you?

A lie? A farce?
The circle Turns, and truth to tell,
The evil one still reigns,
And he was born in hell.

Perhaps to flow and to slide
With the changing tides is best.
But will we live through, survive
These lonely, desperate tests?

We are embattled, but fight.-
We must fight to live, eat, sleep.
For foreboding darkness gathers
In the circling, treacherous deep.

The world is spinning
Bewilderingly, frightfully so.
We need to fight, to hold on,
Till evil is finally let go.

(Raf Evangelista 16 December 2021)

....

56
Social Redemption For
Cockroaches During 2021 –

It is said nothing is created without a purpose,but I originally had four on my list: cockroaches, mosquitos and flies, and certain types of human insects, primarily politicians, that I couldn't find social justification for.

I had cockroaches near the top my list, until I heard that a farm in China had found some useful purpose for these creatures. Useful! Hmmm! I immediately deleted cockroaches from my list.

Then I happened to watch a video showing a thriving farm in China that breeds those miserable insects for human consumption. Some people find social redemption in anything! Ugh!

On second thought, I immediately placed cockroaches right back up on my list! Right after the human variety of insects! These human insects are not even fit for consumption!

So there! (REE, 2 Jan 2021)

....

57
A Call For Change In Mindset

Filipinos must start condemning the "petty, personal attacks" that have become rife in Philippine politics. They must call on government officials, starting with President Duterte, to follow the examples of our great Filipino Statesmen of yesteryears who raised and debated issues, rather than personalities: Presidents Quezon, Osmena, Senators Recto and Diokno, among others.

The season of divisiveness in the country has become so deep that it is critical that we reject what has become far too common in our country: name calling, petty personal attacks, doing and saying whatever it takes just stay in power or to get one's way in politics.

It is dangerous to continue to do so, specially when we are exposed not just internal, but more specially to external threats, the likes of which the Philippines has not seen since Imperial Japan tried to impose on Southeast Asia it's much proclaimed "Japanese Co-Prosperity Sphere." The Belt-Road program of China and its 9 Yard Dash Line in the South China Sea clearly proclaims China's intention to take over Southeast Asia and beyond, darkly echoing what Imperial Japan tried to do 80 years ago.

To continue to be so divided as a people not only lessens who we are as a country, but also stops us from recognizing fully as one nation the kind of threat China poses for the Philippines today. There must be a better way forward. We can work with people who are different from us. We can be friends with people who are different from us. We can love and care about people who are different than us. We can keep people who are different than us safe. We can be good people who care deeply about each other even when we disagree.

We can start by listening to someone with a different opinion—listening not to rebut or debate, but listening to understand. We can articulate our own opinions and beliefs without believing or saying that someone else's are, therefore, wrong. We can embrace difference while seeking common ground.

Trolling one another, fighting one another on social media or any other kind of media is simply not the answer.

We must all agree to "double down" on such an inclusive approach, vowing to represent the Filipino people "not by calling names or playing political games, but by showing up and doing the work to keep Philippines moving forward."

We must all reflect on the legacy left behind by our hero statesmen who dedicated their lives for a united and greater Philippines, among them our martyrs Josefa Escoda, Jose Abad Santos and Vicente Lim. Removing their legacies and rewriting/revising our country's history diminishes Filipinos as a people and the Philippines as a country.

Unity may be the only way we can survive the double whammy of external and internal threats that China, Ineptitude and Corruption of Government, the Pandemic, Typhoons like Odette,Poverty, Joblessness and Despair pose for the Philippines.

If the Leaders will not lead, let the People do so. After all, Sovereignty resides with them! (REE, 24 December 2021)

....

58
Shaking of Hands

Dr Anthony Fauci, America's medical frontliner in the fight against COVID 19, has recommended that the practice of shaking hands should stop permanently because it can spread diseases.

It is interesting that the late Alejandro "Anding" Roces, the former Secretary of Education, insisted more than 20 years ago that shaking hands is one of the most unhealthy and unsanitary habits that we have emulated from the West.

Anding himself chose to greet people, including close friends, Thai style, hands together in prayerful position accompanied with a bow.

Filipinos have started their own contactless greeting with the placing of one's right open palm over the heart, accompanied with a bow of respect.

Both the Thai and Filipino styles of greeting are both elegant and respectful. The bow, like the Japanese way of greeting, denotes respect. But the Thai add the prayerful gesture of the hands, palm to palm, an elegant gesture that means to join in friendship. The Filipino gesture of hand over the heart can mean friendship as well, or beyond that, love.

Of course, both the Thai and Filipino greeting are safe and is not a conduit of illnesses.

And since our grandchildren can no longer as a rule make Mano to their grandparents because of COVID, we can and should teach them an alternative Filipino way of greeting to show respect and love for their elders: hand over the heart and a bow from the waist in greeting. Our youth should not be allowed to lose the beautiful Filipino trait of showing love and respect for their elders.

I agree with both Dr Fauci and Secretary Roces. Let us do away with the shaking of hands during this times of the Pandemic.

(REE, 9 April 2020)

....

59
Sunrise At Sundown

Look to the brilliant
Sunrise at sundown.
The Temple shook
And the curtain was
Rent in two, and the
Darkness reigned.

The cry was heard
"Eli, Eli Lama Sabachthanl," and
Then the last words,
"Consummatum est! "
They rolled the stone,
And sealed His tomb.

Night set in, but

Then the Sun rose
Amidst the darkness
With light of His Love,
And there was but
The empty tomb.
Sunrise pierced
The dark when
He Rose from the grave
To set us free, and
Even angels rejoiced
For the Sun had risen.

The Sun is risen
From the grave!
The Sun is risen!
Hallelujah to the King!
Hallelujah, They sang!

(Raffy Evangelista 4 April 2021)

....

60

Is The Philippines A Part Of China's Continental Shelf? China May Be Planning To Claim It Is!

I wrote this in April 2015. Am reposting to share:

Is The Philippines A Part Of China's Continental Shelf? China May Be Planning To Claim It Is!

The Unclos 200 mile exclusion zone is calculated from a country's continental shelf. We claim that China is building all these islands in the Spratlys and other areas within the West Philippine Sea far beyond the 200 mile exclusion zone of what the rest of the world considers is China's continental shelf, the shelf jutting from the mainland.

But what if China is not following the same calculations as the rest of the world? Remember China is claiming almost all of the China Sea, including what we call the West Philippine Sea, as part of the territory of China, independent of Unclos. In making this claim of ownership, China makes no reference either to Unclos or its continental shelf. Could it be that China's real intention in building and reclaiming islands in this area is so that it can later claim that its continental shelf starts with these islands, and the 200 mile exclusion zone should be calculated from them?

Using this formula, the Philippines could end up in a struggle with China on where China's continental shelf ends and where the Philippine continental shelf begins. The Philippines could very well lose all the seas along our western seaboard to a stronger and more powerful China. And China's claims may even go beyond our western coasts!

Indeed, extending this thesis, could China claim that the land mass of the Philippines, or a portion of it, particularly Luzon and the Benham Rise, are part of China's continental shelf? If China is claiming the entire "China Sea" as an "inland" sea that is part of the mainland, it does not take great leaps of logic to arrive at the possibility that China will also claim that its continental shelf starts at the boundaries of that "inland sea" comprised by the island chain it claims to own. This notion for now seems extremely far fetched. But then who would have imagined that just a few years ago China would claim all of the "China Sea" and start building islands within "spitting" distance of the Philippines.

I remember a meeting in 1977 I had in HongKong when I resided there before its return to Mainland China. My meeting was with an official from the Mainland. He told me then that China had territorial claims not only to the Philippine seas but also to its territory. Bob Romulo, the former Secretary of Foreign Affairs, also told me of a similar incident. Bob told me that during his father's time,

China's Chou En Lai told his father, Carlos P Romulo, that the Philippines is part of China. I have never been able to personally confirm this statement attributed to Chou En Lai.

But what is happening today in our seas seems be an assertion and implementation by China of those claims. The Philippines could be surprised one day to find China claiming the resource rich Benham Rise in the Pacific Ocean off the Quezon and Aurora side and eastern seaboard of the Philippines as part of its continental shelf. Should all countries whose territories are bounded by the "China Sea" be put on notice that their territorial integrity may, even now, be at peril?

Rafael E Evangelista 29 April 2015

(Rafael Evangelista is a Retired Capital Partner of the International Law Firm of Baker & McKenzie)

....

61
Sharing something I sent this to my 83 yr old sister, Rhona, who lives in California.

I wrote this after the attacks on Asian Americans increased in numbers in the United States. –

Sis:

Filipinos who have taken on US citizenship are rightly called Asian Americans. But unlike other Asians from other Asian countries, many Fil Ams may be more than ordinary Asian Americans.

The Philippines was a colony of the United States until 1946, when the Philippines was granted its independence from the United States. All Filipinos who lived from the onset of colonization by the US until the grant of independence in 1946 were American nationals.

They carried US passports. There were no Philippine passports during that period.

Dad and Mom, you, Gene and I were by law American nationals. Some may argue that being American nationals did not make us US citizens. I argue to the contrary. Filipinos who lived during that period could not be law be considered stateless. By law, there was only US citizenship that was available to Filipinos of that era. Hence, we were issued US passports. It is citizenship that determines the state of a person, and the passports issued were recognition of citizenship. We were also American nationals, which in turn determined our nationality.

What about our children? I maintain that under the US Constitution a case can be made that they too were US citizens. The US Constitution provides that children born of US citizens are themselves US citizens. If I am correct in my proposition that you, Gene and I are both US nationals and US citizens, a nationality and citizenship we never voluntarily renounced, then our children by right are US citizens.

Just thought I would toss these ideas into the pot to titillate your thoughts about Fil Ams.

Btw, Filipinos had settlements in several places of the United States even before the arrival of the Pilgrims!

Think about it!

Your brother,

Raf March 5, 2021

....

62
AMDG

Be an achiever: plan purposefully, prepare prayerfully, proceed positively, pursue persistently. In all things, act! There is no advancement if one stands in trepidation, scared to do what one ought to. Always remember that that when one has to sail through deep waters, God is always there to hold our hand. Always remember that the greatest opportunity comes in being and doing good. There is less competition in doing good and a lot more opportunity. Always remember that the freedoms we have today are courtesy of those who came before and were willing to fight for them. Remember that in acting, we are able to achieve. And, always, always, act for the greater glory of God. For there is no greater gift to us than to act for and in God's Glory! Ad Majorem Dei Gloriam! AMDG! (REE, 19 March 2021)

....

63
Me, And My Shadow

Shadows will not dance
In the midst of sunlight.
Flame will not cast its own
Shadow upon nearby walls.
There are times, it seems,
That I have walked and
Have cast no shadows
And not been seen at all.
Blending, melding into
The forest's evergrowth,
Have I been a flame or
Am I just a shadow as
I round the bend of life?
I have been following the
Trail of steps that mark
The path that I trek on.
Will anyone notice the
Footmarks that I leave?

There are times looking back
I see a solitary flame darting
Amidst moving shadows,
A light of long time ago.
I wonder if it was me that
Traveled those distant
Disappearing trails with the
Light of once upon a time.
How I am tempted to
Shout to High Heavens,
"That was me!
That Was really me!"
But then the question
Comes back to haunt me:
"Was it?"

(Raffy Evangelista, 24 July 2021)

....

64
The Road I Travel

Lord, I ask You to be my sentinel,
Let me travel Your Road of Love.
To do whatever it is that You will,
Please guide from me from above.

Light in the deepest darkness
Will still brilliantly shine through.
Take my hand, my heart, my Lord.
Let Your Light lead me to You.

Years have come and gone.
So much time I wasted on me.
Let me focus on the journey
Of Love You want me to see.

Though strong winds buffet me,
Distant skies are still bright blue
The storms will soften and go.
I know You will see me through.

I see the far off gates of
Heaven Where many friends have gone.
I know that is where I will go
When all breath in life is done.

Guide me always from above
To do whatever it is that You will.
I will travel on Your Road my Lord,
Even if I sometimes stumble still.

Show me Your Way, My Lord
Take my hand, my heart in Yours.
Steer me to be Heaven bound
And keep me on Your Course.
I love You, Lord!

(Raffy Evangelista, 18 October 2021)

....

65
I Will Not Be Caged From The Truth

In search for truth,
I will not let my teeth
Cage in my speech,
Nor my lips shut
Out my thoughts.
My tongue will
Speak what I

Believe and feel.
Only the truth
Will hold me back,
As only the truth
Will push me front.

It takes courage
Most times for
The heart and
Mind to speak
In tandem with
The truth, and
Know what is
That is is what
Truly counts.
So in service of
God and County,
I Shall speak the truth.

And I shall
Not hold back,
But act as my
Heart and soul
Shall guide me.
My teeth, and
Lips and tongue
Shall not lock me
Out in silence…
And neither will
Anyone or anything else…
Ever!

(Raffy Evangelista 21 October 2021)

....

66

Great Servant Leaders, Living Reminders Of Our Pledge

Do We Sing
The Words that follow,
And Mean them?
They are A PLEDGE.
Do NOT Sing them
If You Do NOT
Mean Them!-
Lupang hinirang,
Duyan ka ng magiting:
Chosen land,
Cradle of the brave!
Sa manlulupig di ka pasisiil:
Let no conqueror oppress you.
Aming ligaya na 'pag
may mangaapi, ay
mamatay ng dahil sa iyo:
It will be our joy,
in the face of oppression,
to give up our lives for you.
Sa manlulupig di ka pasisiil –
It matters not if the conqueror/oppressor
is foreign or HOMEGROWN.

Be prepared to lay down your lives for love of Country, our Duyan ng Magiting, in the fight against ANY oppressor!

There are those who would betray our Country to domestic and foreign oppressors! Avoid them!

Shun them! Our national elections are not a simple matter of electing leaders. We must choose our leadership during critical times when our Country's freedom, autonomy and independence are threatened. We must make that choice by referring to certain specific criteria, the most basic of which is faithfulness to the Pledge that all of us make from our childhood.

Our greatest leaders have sung those very words as a solemn pledge to serve the Philippines and the Filipino people. Not only have they sung them, but they have lived them by quietly and nobly serving the people in heart, word and deed. All for God and Country!

It is a sad testament that not all who have run for national positions in the national elections can truthfully make that claim! We need Servant Leaders to Lead! (Raffy Evangelista, 14 October 2021)

....

67
USAFFE, A BAND OF HEROES

My father,Lolo Apeng, was technically assigned to the 21st Infantry Division, USAFFE, at the time of the onslaught of the Japanese in 1942 in Bataan. And he and the 21st Infantry Division were assigned to an area of Bataan where some of the fiercest battles of the War took place.The 21st Infantry Regiment, 21st Infantry Division (Philippine Army, Reserve), along with 41st Div and 51st Div Regiments (all Philippine Army, Reserve) together with a lone regular US Army unit, the 57th PS comprised of Filipino enlisted men with American NCOs and officers, held the Abucay Line on the eastern side of the Bataan peninsula (II Corps AOR) from January 9-23, 1942.

This major action happened after the Battle of Layac Junction, which was the first delaying action against the Japanese attempt to penetrate the Bataan Peninsula. The maps available depict the action in Layac Junction and the Abucay Line. It is interesting to note that the so-called poorly-trained, newly-mobilized USAFFE Divisions, with the exception of the lone all-American infantry unit, the 31st Regiment, and the 26th & 57th PS Regiments, were committed as the vanguard to check the Japanese initial advance into Bataan.

However, the truth is, those were all the fighting units they had. The other USSAFE Divisions, regular and reserve, were on the western side of Bataan. The other remaining all-American fighting units that were held in reserve were the 4th Marine Regiment, which was initially held in Corregidor as beach defense (some were also held south in the Bataan rear CP and Mariveles as base security), and the provisional infantry battalions comprised of former US Army Air Corps and Naval units (without planes and ships).

Regardless, history points out that despite the fact the Abucay Line was eventually abandoned, the Japanese suffered heavy casualties, making them re-think their way forward. Except for Japanese attempts to flank I Corps AOR via landings on the west coast of Bataan (which failed), the Battles of the Pockets and the Points (where the Japanese also suffered tactical defeats), no successful major action was made by the Japanese until their main and final offensive beginning April 1942.

By that time, the Filipino-American defenders were exhausted, starved and diseased, their numbers reduced by massive casualties. In the final analysis, the Filipino-American defenders lost a logistics battle and not because they were tactically inferior or less courageous than the Japanese. That, despite what others have noted as inadequacies in equipment, armament, food and medicine,they would have fought to the bitter end had they the means.

There is no doubt in my mind that my father, Lolo Apeng, marched and fought with heroes, the Filipinos who served in the USAFFE. As fate would have it, these Filipino veterans were subjected to the insidious provisions of the infamous US Recission Act of 1956, the law that deprived all USAFFE Filipinos of recognition and honor for their role in WW II.

Raffy Evangelista Proud Son of a WW II Hero and Veteran, Dr. Rafael L Evangelista (Updated, 8

December 2021, in Recogniton of the Anniversary of the Bombing of Pearl Harbor and Manila)

....